THE HISTORY OF MOTOWN

AFRICAN-AMERICAN ACHIEVERS

THE HISTORY OF MOTOWN

Virginia Aronson

CHELSEA HOUSE PUBLISHERS
Philadelphia

Chelsea House Publishers
Editor in Chief Sally Cheney
Production Manager Pamela Loos
Director of Photography Judy Hasday
Art Director Sara Davis
Managing Editor James D. Gallagher
Senior Production Editor J. Christopher Higgins

Staff for THE HISTORY OF MOTOWN
Senior Editor LeeAnne Gelletly
Associate Art Director Takeshi Takahashi
Designer Keith Trego
Picture Researcher Patricia Burns
Cover Designer Takeshi Takahashi

© 2001 by Chelsea House Publishers, a subsidiary of Haights
Cross Communications. All rights reserved. Printed and bound
in the United States of America.

First Printing
3 5 7 9 8 6 4 2

The Chelsea House World Wide Web address is
http://www.chelseahouse.com

Library of Congress Cataloging-in-Publication Data

Aronson, Virginia.
The history of Motown / Virginia Aronson.
  p. cm — (African-American achievers)
Includes bibliographical references (p.) and index.
"Selected Discography": p.
Filmography: p.
ISBN 0-7910-5814-X (alk. paper)
     0-7910-5815-8 (pbk. : alk. paper)
1. Motown Record Corporation—Juvenile literature.
2. Sound recording industry—United States—Juvenile
literature [1. Motown Record Corporation. 2. Gordy, Berry.
3. Sound recording industry.] I. Title. II. Series.
ML3792.A76 2000
781.644'09774'34—dc21
                                    00-045154

CONTENTS

AFRICAN-AMERICAN ACHIEVERS

THE HISTORY OF MOTOWN

1

Ain't Too Proud to Beg

Using $800 in loans from family and friends, entrepreneur Berry Gordy Jr. founded the Motown Record Corporation in 1959, building it up by the mid-1970s into the largest black-owned firm in the United States.

ON JUNE 29, 1988, a legend changed hands when Berry Gordy Jr., founder of Motown Records, sold his company to MCA Records for $61 million. In his press release the 58-year-old African-American executive said he now realized that Motown had evolved into "an American institution." The statement continued, "It is the nature of institutions to take on their own life and to outgrow the individuals who create them. I am proud that this African-American heritage has been embraced by the world and has become permanently woven into the fabric of popular culture."

The sound of Motown, the special brand of soulful music produced by the talented musicians at Berry Gordy's company, first infiltrated the United States during the 1960s with race riots, public protests, and street demonstrations as background noise. The "Motown Sound"—a combination of gospel, pop, rhythm-and-blues, jazz, doo-wop, and country that was created and performed by black artists—captivated the country. It soon circled the globe, uniting people of all ages, races, and classes. Merging gospel-infused vocals with pop music enlivened by raucous horns and percussion, the vibrant Motown Sound crackled with energy. Over a 10-year period Motown produced almost 80 Top 10 records, an achievement unmatched by any other record company in history. (The Top 10 list comes from *Billboard* magazine's "Hot 100" chart, which ranks America's most popular singles, based on weekly sales and record play.) Under Berry Gordy's direction, Motown scored more than 100 number one hits before its sale in 1988.

Motown Records began in 1959 with an $800 loan and a dream. Berry Gordy carefully and creatively built it into an empire that became the most famous record company in the world and one of the most successful black-owned businesses in history. By the time of its sale to MCA Records—almost 30 years after its creation—Motown Records had shaped the course of history by helping to shatter long-standing color barriers in the American entertainment industry. The African-American artists who recorded for Motown became pop stars who were worshiped and swooned over by both black *and* white fans. The Motown Sound became known as "the Sound of Young America." It touched the hearts and joined the hands of music lovers all over the world.

The history of Motown is the story of one man's personal vision. It is the projects-to-riches tale of an African-American dropout from inner-city Detroit, Michigan, a visionary who made hit records in his quest to cultivate a sound that could bring people together. Berry Gordy *is* Motown, and the Motown legend is a fascinating saga of one man's contribution to the multicolored fabric of popular culture.

The first Berry Gordy was Motown Berry Gordy's grandfather, the illegitimate son of a Georgian slave owner named Jim Gordy and a slave named Esther Johnson. Unlike many slaves in the 1860s, Berry was taught to read and write. He grew up to be a shrewd, well-respected businessman, a successful cotton farmer who owned hundreds of acres of land, a general store, and a blacksmith shop. His son Berry II, one of nine children, was a proverbial chip off the old block, a bright, business-minded child with natural leadership ability. When his father was fatally struck by lightning, 24-year-old Berry II took over the family operations, successfully protecting the Gordy property from unlawful seizure by scheming white businessmen.

In 1918, 30-year-old Berry II married 19-year-old Bertha Ida Fuller, an energetic schoolteacher who encouraged his expanding business ventures. But in 1922 Berry Gordy II earned a little too *much* money when he sold a load of his plantation timber for $2,600. At the time, this was a huge sum of cash for a black person to have. To protect their windfall and their lives in a state known for regularly lynching black men, Berry II left Georgia. He followed his brother John up north and settled in Detroit before sending for his wife and three young children: Esther, Fuller, and George.

In the 1920s, Detroit was a city of opportunity for African Americans. "Motor City" was the home of the Ford Motor Company, the auto industry's largest employer of black workers. Ford paid the highest wages of any automaker and offered the widest range of job opportunities to black employees. Even though Berry II chose not to work for Ford, instead carrying on in his family's entrepreneurial tradition, he knew that he could make a good life for the Gordy family in Detroit.

By the time Berry Gordy Jr. (who was actually the third Berry Gordy) was born on November 28, 1929, Berry II had established himself as a professional plasterer and carpenter, and he owned a small grocery store. When Berry Jr. was six, "Pops" opened a larger grocery store named after Booker T. Washington, the famous African-American educator and social reformer. Eventually, Pops also operated a neighborhood printing shop.

During the Black Migration of the 1920s, hundreds of thousands of African Americans traveled from the South in search of jobs in the North. Many, like Berry Gordy's father, were drawn to industrial centers like the "Motor City" of Detroit, Michigan.

Bertha Gordy was the busy mother of eight children, but she still found the time to graduate from the Detroit Institute of Commerce. She then cofounded the Friendship Mutual Life Insurance Company, which specialized in selling insurance policies to African-American families. At home Bertha stressed the importance of education, encouraging self-discipline and focus in her offspring.

From an early age all the children helped out with the family businesses and learned well the Gordy philosophy of hard work and family unity. The girls—Loucye, Esther, Anna, and Gwen—and the boys—Fuller, George, and Robert (the youngest)—worked diligently in school and at the jobs that Pops and Bertha assigned to them. But right from the start, the next-to-youngest child, Berry Gordy Jr., was different.

Young Berry despised manual labor, and he was the only Gordy to bring home poor grades. In school, where Berry had become the class clown, his credo was, "No gag too big, no laugh too small." Intrigued by the illegal gambling operations running in his neighborhood, Berry preferred to develop his street smarts. By the age of 13 he considered himself "the black sheep of the family—mischievous, terrible in school, always in trouble." But Berry was cocky and self-confident. He had a deep passion, "a burning desire to be special, to win, to be somebody." Inspired and nurtured by his ambitious and loving family, he grew more and more confident in himself.

As much as Berry despised the physical grind of plastering and the intellectual demands of school-work, he loved the freedom he found in music and dancing; he also relished making money. When he wasn't reluctantly working for Pops, Berry was busy developing his own small businesses: among them, a homemade shoe-shine stand and a daring news-paper route selling black papers in white neighbor-hoods. Berry also supplied the idea, and a talented young friend the voice, for a unique door-to-door singing gig. Whatever money Berry earned he rapidly spent at local clubs and ballrooms, where he was known for his persistence—if not his popular-ity—with the girls.

Another of young Berry's favorite hangouts was the Brewster Center, a local recreational facility for inner-city kids, where the scrappy teenager took up boxing. Amateur boxing teams flourished in Detroit, the city where Joe Louis, the greatest heavyweight of his generation and an African-American hero, learned to fight. Fuller and Robert

Gordy had also tried boxing, but only Berry turned out to possess the natural skill and the burning desire required to compete in such a punishing sport. Against his family's wishes Berry dropped out of the 11th grade to become a professional boxer. He was 16 years old and confident that he would become a champion.

Despite his above-average ability and drive, Berry was not destined for greatness in the ring, primarily because of his small stature. He managed to win 10 out of his 15 pro fights, however, proving to himself and his family that he was indeed a genuine Gordy: motivated, hardworking, and ambitious.

Berry quit the ring in 1950 to pursue his other dream career: songwriting. "Whenever I wasn't at the Brewster Center training I was somewhere writing songs—which no one wanted to hear," Berry recounts in his autobiography, *To Be Loved: The Music, the Magic, the Memories of Motown*. One hot August day when he was training at the gym, Berry noticed two posters displayed together on a pillar, one announcing an upcoming battle of the bands, the other advertising a boxing bout on the same night: "I stared at both posters for some time, realizing the fighters could fight once and maybe not fight again for three or four weeks, or months, or never. The bands were doing it every night, city after city, and not getting hurt. I then noticed the fighters were about twenty-three and looked fifty; the band leaders about fifty and looked twenty-three."

Berry took off his boxing gloves and turned his attention to songwriting.

His first successful endeavor was a one-minute commercial jingle for the Gordy Print Shop, which he wrote and recorded in the basement studio of a local disc jockey. His first full-length song, "You Are You," was inspired by one of his favorite film stars, Doris Day. For $25 Berry had the song published in sheet music form so he could send a copy to the actress. (Forty-three years later Berry met with Doris Day and presented her with a framed copy of the ballad.) But Berry's songwriting career was soon interrupted by the Korean War when he was drafted into the U.S. Army in 1951.

During his two-year stint as a soldier, Berry earned his GED, or high school equivalency degree. While stationed in Korea, he volunteered as a chaplain's assistant. He drove a jeep to the front lines of battle, where he played an organ small enough to fit into a suitcase between hurried religious services for the troops. Upon his discharge in 1953, Berry happily returned to Detroit.

With the money he had saved up from his army pay, plus loans from his father and his business partner and brother, George, Berry opened a record shop in the same family-owned block of buildings that housed the Booker T. Washington General Store and the Gordy Print Shop. The 3D Record Mart specialized in jazz, which Berry had grown to love while frequenting the many jazz clubs that thrived throughout the city.

A mixture of blues, ragtime, spirituals, folk music, and marching music, jazz had emerged in the 1920s as the country's first popular black art form. The big band sound flourished until the 1940s, when a new form of jazz emerged. Bebop, characterized by improvised rhythms and altered chords, gradually eclipsed the big band sound. By the 1950s small combos "jammed" in black clubs throughout the New York City neighborhood of Harlem—and in the neighborhoods of many other cities.

Despite the growing popularity of bebop jazz in all of the hippest Detroit nightspots, most of the black residents in Berry's neighborhood still preferred blues music. Having evolved in the late 19th century from the work songs sung by slaves, blues music came directly from the African-American experience. Influenced by gospel music, the blues is simple in form and deep in feeling, exploring the suffering and pain of human life.

Originally categorized as "race music" in record catalogs, blues music was undergoing a transformation in the 1950s. A more urban sound, known as R&B, or rhythm-and-blues, was emerging. On city street corners groups of kids sang doo-wop, a simplified rhythm-and-blues music characterized by basic melodies and lyrics accentuated with more complex harmonies. In Detroit and elsewhere in the United States, African-American families sat around the piano to sing gospel songs—and the ever popular blues. Jazz, however, had a more limited fan base.

By 1955 the 3D Record Mart had gone out of business, despite Berry's last-minute attempt to stock his store with more popular records by blues artists. Berry emerged from this failure with a budding knowledge of the field of "race music," as well as a deep appreciation for the soulful appeal of the blues. He had also learned the importance of selling people what *they* wanted, rather than what *he* preferred—a lesson that would later underscore his business acumen and songwriting skills.

Before the 3D Record Mart went under, a friend of Berry's dropped in one day accompanied by some young ladies, including a pretty medical worker named Thelma Coleman. A few months after they met, Berry married 19-year-old Thelma. By 1956 the couple had three children: Hazel Joy, Berry IV, and Terry James.

After a stint of selling cookware door-to-door, Berry was forced by the financial demands of his growing family to take an assembly line job at the Ford Motor Company's Lincoln-Mercury automotive plant. For $86.40 a week he fastened upholstery and chrome strips to an endless stream of auto frames passing by on a conveyor belt. Berry supplemented his regular income by working at Ford on the weekends and putting in plenty of

overtime—and by joining a local poker club.

By the mid-1950s poor residents of Detroit no longer viewed the auto industry as a way to move up in the world. The production line work was relentless, monotonous, and even dangerous. "Everybody talked about it, they said it was the house of murder," wrote one assembly line worker about his draining job at the Ford Motor Company. "Every worker could identify Ford workers on the streetcars going home at night. Every worker who was asleep was working for Ford." Berry preserved his energy and his sanity on the auto production line by creating songs in his head while he worked.

In 1957, when he realized that he had to save himself from the mind-numbing drudgery of factory work, Berry left his job at Ford. His wife, however,

With the failure of his first music business—a jazz record shop—Berry turned to a job more typical of the "Motor City." To pay the bills for his growing family, he joined the Ford workers on the auto assembly lines, but he continued to write songs at the same time.

After quitting his factory job, Berry composed songs by day and checked out the local clubs at night, eventually writing songs for some of the performers he met. One popular African-American singer at the time was Sarah Vaughan, nicknamed "the Divine One." Famed for her ability to improvise melodies, Vaughan is said to have defined the bebop style of the 1940s.

was not supportive of his intended switch to a full-time songwriting career. Thelma had grown tired of Berry's failed business ventures, and she could no longer tolerate being married to a dreamer. The couple split up.

Berry worked on his songs during the day and checked out the music scene at night, dressed in a silk suit with his hair "processed" to relax the kinks into smooth waves. At the local clubs he took in memorable performances by such popular African-American singers as Dinah Washington, Sarah Vaughan, and the legendary Billie Holiday. His sisters Gwen and Anna, who owned a photo concession at a hip music club, introduced Berry to the performers they had befriended. In short order Berry was penning songs for some of the artists he had met while out on the town.

When Thelma filed for divorce, Berry moved in with his sister Gwen. As a songwriter-for-hire, he collaborated with Gwen and other rookie writers to create new tunes for budding artists, including "All I Could Do Was Cry," which later became a hit for Etta James. It was Berry's "Reet Petite," however, that was his first chart-topper. He cowrote the song in 1957 for Jackie Wilson, a sexy singer with whom Berry had boxed in the 1940s.

By the time he had written his third hit song for Wilson, Berry had established himself as the most prolific and publishable songwriter in Detroit. But he was still sharing an apartment with his sister—although not Gwen. By this time he had moved in with Loucye. Despite his reputation as a slick dresser and a free spender at the nightclubs around Detroit, Berry was broke. He could write songs that climbed the charts and earned hundreds of thousands of dollars, but he had yet to receive his fair share of the profits from any of his hit tunes.

At the time, popular music was published and distributed primarily by the major record labels. These were largely white-owned companies that promoted the "pop" sound of white singers and overlooked the rhythm-and-blues and rock-and-roll songs by black performers. The major labels controlled all the rights to the records they produced, so when a title did well, their own publishing houses kept most of the earnings. Very little profit filtered down to the performers, writers, and musicians.

Berry began to consider establishing a small record-leasing business to help artists cut their *own* records, then license the songs—for an advance and royalties—to the major labels for distribution. Berry wanted to have more control over his own songs and earnings, and to provide the same opportunity for other black artists.

Berry had already become a manager of performers, putting together a stable of singers to record his songs. He often booked the cheapest studio times at United Sound, Detroit's best-equipped recording studio, where he would record up-and-coming performers late at night. His roster included several young singers who would later become major artists at Motown: future Temptations David Ruffin and Melvin Franklin, and Lamont Dozier, a future Motown songwriter.

When Gwen Gordy established her own record label, Anna Records (named after their sister), she asked Berry to join her and another songwriter in their venture. But Berry knew that he functioned best as his own boss, so he declined Gwen's offer. (Anna Records would later become one of Motown's labels.) Berry knew that if he set up his own record business, he would finally be paid for his efforts. "Songwriting was my love, and protecting that love, in many ways, was the motivation for everything I did in the early years of my career," Berry wrote in his autobiography. "Producing the artists who sang my songs was the next logical step to making sure my songs were done the way I wanted. Protecting my songs was also the reason I got into publishing and eventually the record business."

In late 1957 Berry formed an important partnership. After listening to the poetic lyrics of a 17-year-old singer and aspiring songwriter named William "Smokey" Robinson, who fronted a band called the Matadors, Berry began to work with this talented young musician. The two friends soon cowrote a song called "Got a Job." At Berry's suggestion the Matadors changed their name to the Miracles, and on February 19, 1958 (Smokey's 18th birthday), their song was released. "Got a Job" became one of the hottest records in town, making the Miracles local stars overnight.

When Berry received his royalty check for cowriting and producing the Miracles' first hit song, he was speechless: it was for just $3.19! His biggest hit song for Jackie Wilson, the classic R&B tune "Lonely Teardrops," had earned him only $1,000 in royalties. "It was wrong, unfair. And on top of that—bad business," Berry wrote in his autobiography about the music business of the late 1950s. "I knew there must be thousands of other writers out there just like me, and all they wanted to do was write songs—and get paid. If I set up a company that did that, I was sure all the writers would come to me."

Smokey Robinson understood his friend's frustration only too well, and he encouraged Berry to establish his own music production and publishing company. "Why work for the man? Why not *be* the man?" he suggested.

Berry turned to his family once more for a business loan. He was 29 years old, a divorced father of three who lived with his sister and earned about $30 a week. The Gordys were understandably reluctant to lend Berry the $800 he needed to put out his first record. But Berry was passionate, committed, and—as always—extremely convincing. A family meeting was held and the decision was unanimous: Berry Gordy got his money. Motown, the black music business that would forever change the sound of American pop, was about to be born.

Another well-known singer of the 1950s was Jackie Wilson, whom Berry had once fought against in the boxing ring. When his hit song for Wilson, "Lonely Teardrops," earned Berry just $1,000 in royalties, he decided to take charge of the production of his own artistic efforts.

2

Ain't No Mountain High Enough

THE FIRST RECORD Berry Gordy wrote, produced, published, and released himself was "Come to Me," a churchy R&B song he created with a charismatic young Detroit singer named Marv Johnson. Smokey helped record the song at United Sound. Also on hand was a spunky backup vocal group Berry had put together. The Rayber Voices consisted of a petite 21-year-old with perfect pitch named Raynoma Liles and Berry (hence the combination of *Ray* and *ber*), as well as two future Motown songwriters named Brian Holland and Robert Bateman and several other singers. Berry chose the commercial-sounding name Tamla for his record label, and the song was published by his music publishing company, which he had dubbed Jobete, a blending of his three children's names (*Jo* from Joy, *be* from Berry, and *te* from Terry).

In the days before complicated postproduction requirements delayed record releases by a year or more, producers could record a song in one night and have a record out on the street the very next day. Marv Johnson's new song was an immediate local hit. Berry quickly sold the record to United Artists, which distributed the hot single across the United States. "Come to Me" climbed to number 30 on *Billboard*'s Top 100 hits list in the spring of

Berry named the headquarters for his new record company "Hitsville U.S.A." Located in midtown Detroit, the two-story bungalow soon became home to a hit-making machine. Modeled after an auto factory plant, the music production company included departments for "quality control" and "artist development."

1959; it remained there for six weeks.

Berry had been operating his business out of his sister Gwen's apartment, where Anna Records was also based, when Raynoma offered her three-room home as a headquarters for Berry's budding company. Ray was by this time Berry's devoted assistant, sharing her impressive technical skills and musical training. Her ability to write out lead sheets, the detailed drafts of new songs (on sheet music, with the melodies, chords, and lyrics note for note), proved indispensable to Berry. Ray had also fallen madly in love with him; over time Berry's appreciation of his assistant turned into romance. Although they eventually married, their partnership would be brief and rocky, the first of many sometimes-romantic, sometimes-platonic collaborations with women that Berry would form throughout his Motown career.

Over the next year Berry produced two hits for Marv Johnson that climbed into the Top 10. When he cut a red-hot song with the Miracles called "Bad Girl," Berry decided to launch a new label, "something that would capture the feeling of my roots—my hometown," he later explained. As a tribute to the Motor City of Detroit, Berry named his new record label—and later his record company—Motown.

Record companies typically establish more than one label for the music they produce, sometimes to create different identities that will attract a variety of listeners, or to feature the work of a specific producer or artist. In the early 1960s another reason to market a variety of labels was to get maximum airplay; at the time, many radio stations avoided appearing to play favorites with one particular label. After Tamla and Motown, Berry's subsequent labels included Rayber, Melody, Miracle, Soul, Gordy, and Jazz Workshop for jazz singles. But 1959's "Bad Girl" proved too costly for Berry to distribute himself, so his first Motown record was still to come.

By this time Ray's apartment was far too small for the growing business—especially since Berry was also living there with Ray and her young son, Cliff. After Ray and Berry's son, Kerry, was born, they began to search for a larger space that could serve as both their home and the Motown offices.

It was Ray who found the modest two-story house at 2648 West Grand Boulevard, a tree-lined street in the mid-Detroit area. The bungalow-style house was comfortably situated in the local black community. This would help to establish Berry's enterprise as the neighborhood record company, a place that welcomed singers, musicians, songwriters, and other types of local talent to stop in. Eventually a weekly audition was scheduled to channel the steady flow of aspiring artists.

The house had an extra-large picture window in front and a former photography studio in the back that Berry could convert into a tiny recording studio. He pronounced the building "perfect for my growing operation," and hung a huge sign out front above the picture window, proclaiming it "Hitsville U.S.A." At the time Berry explained, "That's the only name I can think of that expresses what I want it to be—a hip name for a factory where hits are going to be built."

The Gordys all pitched in to help Berry fix up the old building. They painted the place white with black trim, sealed up the cracks, and installed soundproofing material. The ground floor was converted into a lobby and control room; the top floor into a music room, offices, and living quarters for Berry, Ray, and the two children.

Then, once Hitsville was open for business, most of the Gordys stayed on to assist Berry with its day-to-day operations. His sister Esther and her accountant husband, George Edwards, worked in an upstairs bedroom that had been converted into a bookkeeping office. In another upstairs office

Loucye developed the company's manufacturing department to handle record production, billing, and shipping, as well as graphics and liner notes. Brother George produced songs; Fuller eventually handled personnel and company policy. Robert would run Jobete Music Publishing for 20 years, and both of Berry's parents became intimately involved in the business as advisers. Ray worked in the music publishing department, assisted by her brother and Janie Bradford, the company's first receptionist.

Family took precedence in Berry's evolving corporate structure. In addition to the Gordy family, the expanding staff of artists and business personnel became the "Motown family." Talented individuals were drawn to Hitsville's uniquely supportive and creative atmosphere. Local kids hung around on the front lawn, singing and dancing, hoping to be discovered. Some dared to venture inside Hitsville to apply for jobs as secretaries, office helpers, and janitors. Martha Reeves answered the phone at Hitsville early on—one of many young receptionists who patiently awaited an opportunity to show off their musical talents.

Berry ruled his company like a gentle, but demanding, patriarch. He allowed his artists and other employees to experiment creatively, pushing them to both compete and cooperate with one another as they strived to fulfill their individual potential. He forbade misbehavior—excessive drinking, drug use, wild partying, or goofing off— and attempted to instill in his talent a strong sense of dignity, pride, and confidence.

Monday-morning staff meetings were held in the studio, and all employees attended. After discussing business, everybody sang the company song. The company cook, "Miss Lilly" Hart, prepared lunch daily for everyone who wanted it. Frequent picnics, barbecues, and parties featured artists entertaining one another between intense games of cards, touch football, volleyball, baseball, and footraces.

"Motown was a family, right from the beginning—living together, playing together, making music together, eating together," recounts Berry in *To Be Loved*. "In many ways Hitsville was like growing up in the Gordy family—fierce closeness and fierce competition and constant collaboration." For Berry Gordy, family meant hard work, discipline, and unity. Motown functioned like a close-knit and talented family, its members fighting often, laughing a lot, and loving what they were doing.

Hitsville quickly became the hit factory Berry had envisioned, a creative assembly line of musicians and management who pumped out hit song after hit song. Using the mass production techniques he had observed during his long, dull days at the Lincoln-Mercury plant, Berry organized Motown so that it ran like an efficient factory. "I wanted a place where a kid off the street could walk in one door an unknown and come out another a recording artist—a star," Berry later stated about his company design. Yet Berry also recognized the uniqueness of each individual, working with his artists to develop their special talents and help them reach—and often far surpass—their own goals.

As the head of Motown, Berry demanded exclusive ownership of all songs recorded by the company and sole management of the artists he employed. But he was also extraordinarily generous with his employees: he shared ample amounts of his time, his creative input, and, eventually, Motown's massive earnings. Unlike other music production companies, Motown allowed black artists to earn their fair share of the profits. Many at Motown became wealthier and more famous than they had ever dreamed possible.

"Money (That's What I Want)" was one of the first records cut in Hitsville's little recording studio. Berry wrote the song with input from the feisty

Nineteen-year-old Mary Wells, the company's first solo super-star, recorded the first Motown label release, "Bye Bye Baby." By 1962, three of her songs were at the top of the charts, thanks to the talents of Berry's friend Smokey Robinson, who wrote and produced all three.

receptionist, Janie Bradford, who contributed the memorable line "Your love gives me such a thrill, / but your love don't pay my bills." Barrett Strong belted out the driving R&B dance tune, with the Rayber Voices supplying the resounding chorus, "That's what I want."

After the single was well received locally as a Tamla label release, Berry put "Money" on his sister's Anna Records label in order to market it nationally through Gwen's distributors. This proved to be a costly error: Berry soon discovered that he had earned more money from his own local sales than from all of the national distributors! A Top 40 song for eight straight weeks in the spring of 1960, "Money" was making top dollar, but Berry was still flat broke. "On my next record I knew I had to go for it by myself—national all the way," Berry recalled.

By the fall Smokey Robinson had come up with a potential hit for Hitsville. But when the Miracles' "Shop Around" was first released as a Tamla single, Berry realized that something was terribly wrong: the song sounded deathly slow. Berry telephoned Smokey at three o'clock in the morning, begging him to collect the rest of the Miracles and come over to the studio to cut the song again.

Berry sat in for the piano player, who failed to show up for the impromptu predawn session, and the groggy team woke up enough to put together a more spirited version of "Shop Around." By the end of the year, Motown had scored its first million-selling record when "Shop Around" hit the number two spot on the Top 10 hits list, where it remained for 13 weeks. By selling 1 million copies, the single earned the company its first gold record. "Shop Around" was a landmark for Berry, a crossover success that appealed to all of teenage America—urban and suburban, male and female, white and black.

The Miracles were Motown's first Top 10 hit makers, but the company's first solo superstar was Mary Wells, a 19-year-old singer with a seductive voice. She had initially captured Motown's attention with a song she wrote for Jackie Wilson, but Berry quickly decided that he preferred the teen's smooth, sophisticated voice and asked her if she would like to record it herself. "Until Motown, in Detroit, there were three big careers for a black girl," Mary Wells said later, "babies, the factories, or day work." After recording the modestly successful "Bye Bye Baby"—the first Motown label release—the talented young singer was able to quit her job helping her mother scrub floors. By 1962 Wells was at the top of the charts with such hits as "The One Who Really Loves You," "You

Beat Me to the Punch," and "Two Lovers." Smokey Robinson wrote and produced all three songs.

The Marvelettes were Berry's first hot female group. They were four high school girls who provided Motown with its second million-seller and first number one pop-chart hit, "Please Mr. Postman." Based on a song written in one night by group member Georgia Dobbins, who later dropped out, "Please Mr. Postman" was produced by a pair of singer-songwriters named *Brian* Holland and R*obert* Bateman. "Brianbert" also contributed to the Marvelettes' follow-up hits "Twistin' Postman" and "Playboy."

Just as Smokey Robinson had teamed up with Mary Wells to create her hit songs, other Motown artists were collaborating on tunes, lyrics, arrangements, and presentation. Berry had established what he called "quality control," a system he cleverly adapted from the management style employed by Detroit's automotive companies. Producers would submit their new "product" to the quality control department, where at a weekly meeting "product evaluation" would take place. Every Friday morning Motown employees—including the sales force and the office help—would listen to and score the latest sample recordings, discussing their views (often heatedly) before voting on whether or not each song should be released.

Berry believed that these meetings were crucial to the success of Motown. He knew as well as everybody else that careers depended on the choices made on those tense Friday mornings. He advised his talent to work together to create the best songs, surefire hits that quality control would readily approve. The system he developed fostered the driving, competitive spirit and the creative unity that made Motown grow and prosper. His quality control system worked. Berry and his employees—singers and secretaries, songwriters

Discovered at a talent show at Inkster High School in Detroit, the Marvelettes provided Motown with its first number one pop-chart hit, "Please Mr. Postman."

and salesmen—readily recognized the emerging hits of the 1960s and 1970s. They selected the cream of the crop, and single after single rapidly rose to the top of the pop charts.

In the autumn of 1962, with a handful of hit songs and several popular acts on its roster, Motown went on the road. Berry's Motortown Revue (later called the Motown Revue) was an original concept. Although touring revues had been a rock-and-roll staple since 1950, they were usually organized by radio deejays or the stars themselves to generate public interest. Motown became the first record company in history to invest wisely in what later became known as "tour support" to build its artists' marketability and fan base.

On a cold October morning Berry waved good-bye as some two dozen young black artists piled into the caravan of a bus and five cars that would take them on a grueling, exciting 10-week tour of the United States. The Motortown Revue was scheduled to kick off the trip with shows at the Howard Theatre in Washington, D.C., followed by a series of one-night performances throughout the still-segregated South. It would wrap up with a 10-day engagement at the famed Apollo Theatre in New York City. This large Harlem showplace was widely regarded as the most prestigious venue for African-American entertainers. If they were well received at the Apollo, performers knew that they had reached the pinnacle of success in black entertainment.

On the road Thomas "Beans" Bowles, baritone saxophonist and flute player for the Hitsville backup band, served as tour manager for Motown headliners the Miracles, Mary Wells, the Marvelettes, and Marv Johnson. Beans was also responsible for the lesser-known Motown acts, including the Contours, secretary Martha Reeves and her up-and-coming group, the Vandellas, and stage-shy Marvin Gaye. The giddy performers—most of whom had never been outside of Michigan—were accompanied by three chaperones. One of these watchful adults was Mrs. Ernestine Ross, the mother of Diane, a member of the high school–aged Supremes. By the end of the following year, every one of the Motortown Revue performers would score at least one Top 40 hit. "We had no idea in the world where we were really off to," admitted one of the Contours years after taking the Motortown Revue's road to fame and fortune.

The novice troupe performed at clubs and theaters on what was known as "the chitlin circuit": places that welcomed African-American entertainers to appear before mostly black audiences. Following a date at the Boston Arena on November 2, the revue hit 19 cities in 23 days, including 15 performance dates in the Deep South.

The Motown artists found their first national tour both thrilling and exhausting. Bandleader Choker Campbell later said that the young artists suffered from a widespread case of nerves, "not knowing what the road was like. They had never been out there before." Rules governing behavior were strict, especially for the female artists. They were warned to stay away from the older, more experienced backup musicians—mostly men in their twenties and thirties who were not unfamiliar with whiskey and marijuana. The Motown acts lacked polish onstage, a sore point that was not lost on Berry whenever he showed up to observe a revue performance.

The members of the revue were concerned about their reception in the South, where civil

In the fall of 1962 Motown became the first record company to send its artists on tour—to perform at venues in the South and along the East Coast. Included on the Motortown Revue were the Miracles, whose lead singer Smokey Robinson (right) had helped the group produce Motown's first Top 10 hit maker and first million-selling record, "Shop Around."

rights boycotts and sit-ins culminating in violence
were not uncommon, and "whites only" restaurants
and hotels denied entrance to African Americans.
In Birmingham, Alabama, the revue played before a
racially mixed audience. As they boarded the bus
after the show, gunshots were fired in the performers' direction. Mary Wells captured their horror and
sadness when she later recalled, "Me in my little
Motown star bubble. All of a sudden everything
kind of crushes."

The first Motortown Revue was certainly a memorable experience for all the young singers—and a wildly successful endeavor for the rookie record company—but the group was only too happy to return to Detroit for Christmas. While on the road, each of the revue members' earnings had been forwarded to their personal bank accounts in Detroit. Berry devised this system to protect the artists—particularly those who were underage—from squandering their earnings. "We worked that kind of stuff out so they couldn't spend all the money on the road," explained Beans Bowles. In an article published in the *Detroit Free Press* soon after the revue had returned to town, Berry was quoted as saying, "We try to help artists personally with their investment programs so that they don't wind up broke. We are very much concerned with the artist's welfare."

As 1962 drew to a close, Berry's company celebrated the holidays at the first annual Motown Christmas party. It was held at the Greystone Ballroom, a Detroit landmark Berry had purchased earlier in the year. Smokey Robinson won the first annual Motown Spirit Award, one of many he would receive for exemplifying the dogged goodwill and quest for personal excellence that characterized Motown in its earliest years. As Berry recounts in *To Be Loved,* "It was an atmosphere that made you feel no matter how high your goals, they were reachable, no matter who you were. I had always figured that less than 1 percent of all the people in the world reach their full potential. Seeing that potential in others, I realized that by helping them reach theirs, maybe I could reach mine."

The list of Motown artists who benefited from Berry Gordy's vision and evolved into world-famous performers is long and glorious.

3

Superstar (Remember How You Got Where You Are)

LITTLE FREDA PAYNE, a musical prodigy, began hanging around Hitsville before she turned 13. Although Berry had big plans for her career, Motown was unable to create a hit song for the talented youngster. At 18, Payne left Detroit for New York, where she performed with such legendary stars as Pearl Bailey and Duke Ellington. In 1970 she struck gold with the Top 10 hit "Band of Gold." Neither that enormously popular song nor her follow-up hits were on the Motown label.

But there was another child prodigy hanging out at Hitsville in the early days who *did* find fame and fortune with Motown.

As Berry remembers their first meeting, he was eating breakfast in his office when an employee rushed in, crying, "B. G., you got to come hear this little kid *now!*" In the studio a young blind boy was singing and pounding the bongos. He was also playing the harmonica surprisingly well. The 10-year-old dynamo, who had been discovered by the brother of one of the Miracles, soon became the Motown mascot. A natural mimic, Stevland Morris had initiated his own music training by listening to the radio, but at Motown he became a rapt student, quickly learning how to play the drums better and to control his high-pitched voice.

At the age of 12, Little Stevie Wonder made his first recording for Motown—the jazzy tune "Fingertips (Part 2)." It climbed to the top of Billboard's pop charts and became Motown's second number one single. The album 12 Year Old Genius, *which featured this cut, became the first Motown album to reach number one on the pop album charts.*

When the Motortown Revue performed at the Apollo Theatre to close out its first tour, Little Stevie Wonder joined the lineup. (According to Berry, he once remarked, "Boy! That kid's a wonder," and the nickname stuck.) An opening act, Little Stevie bounced from one instrument to another, firing up the audience with his infectious zest and dazzling energy. After 31 shows over a 10-day engagement, the Motortown Revue—and its newest act, Little Stevie Wonder—were undeniably hot. Motown had reached the pinnacle of success in black entertainment.

In 1963 Little Stevie had his first hit song when a mistake was made during the live recording of a revue show in Chicago. After finishing the jazzy tune "Fingertips," Stevie was being led off the stage, when he suddenly bounded back out before the screaming audience and began to perform the song again. His bass player had already left, and Mary Wells's bassist, who was setting up onstage, yelled out, "What key? What key?" Fans loved the genuineness and raw spontaneity so much that "Fingertips (Part 2)" became the number one hit on the *Billboard* pop charts, Motown's second number one single (and the first live single ever to climb into the top slot) as well as the cornerstone for Motown's first number one album.

Little Stevie continually played jokes on his friends at Motown. He could imitate Berry's voice so well that he would often fool the other employees. For instance, he would make phone calls while impersonating Gordy. He would make requests like, "This is Berry and I want you to go get Stevie that tape recorder right away. . . . I'm sure he'll get it back to us in a few days." Discussing the prank years later, Stevie remembered with amusement, "After they fell for this stunt about three times and never got the tape recorder back, they gave me a recorder as a belated birthday present."

Motown was rapidly outgrowing the original Hitsville house, so Berry purchased some neighboring houses in order to expand his operation. "My assembly-line dream was becoming a reality," he recalls in *To Be Loved.* "Not much could thrill me more than walking through the hallways of the various buildings and stopping in on the different creative stations. On a typical day I'd go from one end of the spectrum to the other—songwriting to corporate finance—problem-solving, encouraging, motivating, teaching, challenging, complaining."

One of Berry's biggest complaints was that the acts still lacked professionalism during live performances. To address this problem, he created a new department. The artist development program operated out of a building across from Hitsville, on West Grand Boulevard. The classes were initially coordinated by Berry's strikingly attractive and impeccably groomed sisters Anna and Gwen. But the two former models soon convinced their modeling instructor, Maxine Powell, to take over. Powell was the former owner of Detroit's first finishing school and modeling agency for African Americans.

Motown's very own Miss Manners taught the young black performers how to walk, talk, dress, and behave like professionals—like the stars they were becoming. She would inform her awkward, slump-shouldered, gum-chewing students, "You are going to be good enough to perform for kings," patiently advising them on stage technique and helping them build their grace and self-confidence. "Don't forget, these were kids," Ms. Powell stated in an interview in 1986. "They came from the streets and the projects. They were rude and crude-acting. They didn't know how to look you in the eye or shake hands. They were diamonds in the rough."

Ms. Powell was also responsible for dressing the talent, selecting the colors and styles best suited to each performer. To keep Motown's expenses down, she often improvised by shopping at bridal stores, buying suits on sale and altering them to fit, and adding rhinestones to jackets and shifts by hand. She insisted on bras and girdles for the girls and begged them not to stick out their buttocks when they performed. "They were young and had to be guided into a wholesome way of life," Ms. Powell later explained. She served as a chaperone on the road, keeping the young folks in line and steering them away from alcohol and drugs.

"I know this may sound like I'm patting myself on the back," Maxine Powell later said, "but I never had a tough student. I never got angry and I didn't have any failures. I told the artists what I wanted to do for them, and they were behind me 100 percent. I treated them like top artists, because that's how I saw them."

Berry's ultimate goal was to groom his acts for the big transition from the chitlin circuit to the ritzy and mostly white supper clubs of Las Vegas and New York. Once Motown had made it in African-American entertainment, Berry felt it was time to cross over to the mainstream. He knew that the music Motown was creating appealed to both black and white listeners, so he was determined to catapult his performers into the most visible, best-paying, predominantly white pop-music outlets. He envisioned Motown dominating Dick Clark's *American Bandstand*, network variety shows like *The Ed Sullivan Show*, and New York City's toniest showroom, the Copacabana. Berry saw his up-and-coming talent not just as top African-American performers, but as the world's future superstars.

One of Berry's most unlikely superstars was a coolly intense singer named Marvin Gaye. Although female fans went absolutely crazy for the handsome young man with the sexy, elegant voice, Gaye, the son of a fiery and domineering Pentecostal minister, struggled through his public performances. He was

An early member of Motown, Marvin Gaye recorded on its Tamla label in 1961, the same year he married Berry Gordy's sister Anna. Although Gaye began his career at Motown as a crooner of light romantic ballads, he later moved on to more complex social issues in his work.

painfully shy, panic-stricken onstage, and torn between the pop music that was building his career and a yearning for a more spiritual sound.

In 1961 Gaye had joined the Gordy family when he married Berry's sister Anna, who was 17 years older than the 24-year-old musician. At the time, Gaye's star had yet to rise at Motown, where he served as a session drummer and pianist, humbly remaining in the background. But in 1963 Gaye's catchy dance tune "Hitch Hike" climbed into the Top 40, the first of three hit songs he would release that year. Public acclaim and financial success only served to increase the sensitive singer's discomfort, fueling his obsessive fear that he was somehow selling out.

Martha Reeves, on the other hand, had no such

reservations about stardom. By the time she was four years old, the little girl knew she would one day be a singer—maybe even a star like one of her idols, popular gospel/pop soloist Della Reese. When Berry refused to audition her girl group, the Del-Phis, the determined Reeves applied for an office job at Motown. "I worked two weeks for nothing, I wanted to be there so much," she recalled later.

Reeves and her two girlfriends soon changed their name to the Vels, then to the Vandellas, slowly insinuating themselves into the Motown studio, where they provided backup vocals for some of Marvin Gaye's early recordings. Then Martha got her big break when the increasingly moody Mary Wells failed to show up for a recording session one day. The bold receptionist sat in for the absent star, surprising everyone with her steamy, powerful voice. By the end of 1963, Martha and the Vandellas had scored big with their hot, gospel-based "(Love Is Like A) Heat Wave," and then with "Quicksand," both Top 10 songs.

Before the year's end Berry signed a foreign distribution deal with the record company EMI to market Motown's songs overseas on the international label, Tamla-Motown. The immediate and enormous popularity of Motown music in other countries further confirmed Berry's personal belief that "all people have so much in common. Our music conveyed basic feelings, cutting through cultural and language barriers. It's just a matter of communication. Communication breeds understanding and understanding breeds everything else."

On a personal level, however, Berry was facing two upsetting misunderstandings. His ex-wife Ray had been sent to a New York jail for bootlegging Motown records and selling the songs for her own profit while operating the East Coast branch of Jobete Music Publishing. Although Gordy was shocked and hurt by Ray's disloyal and illegal activities, he eventually forgave her misguided behavior.

Around the same time, Mary Wells sent her lawyer to the Motown offices to disaffirm all of her contracts at the age of majority (21 years old), arguing that her contract was void since she was underage when she signed it. Again, Berry was surprised and hurt by such apparent disloyalty—in this case, from his biggest female star. Wells's perky love song "My Guy" had recently won her international fame when Motown sent her to tour England as the opening act for the Beatles.

Her departure in the wake of her biggest hit was a slap in the face for Motown, yet in an article about Wells's defection published in *Billboard* magazine in July 1964, Motown's head of sales already had her possible successors in mind: "[Barney] Ales, stating that he is aware that many offers are proffered to an artist who has a top record, added that he would like to alert the industry to a group of young ladies called the Supremes, 'who will have the next No. 1 record in the U.S.'"

In fact, *three* Motown acts would end up ruling the pop charts in 1964, joining Marvin Gaye, Little Stevie Wonder, Martha and the Vandellas, the Marvelettes, the Contours, and the Miracles on Hitsville's seemingly endless production line of hit makers. Next up on the roster for fame were the Four Tops, the Temptations, and the most successful female trio in history—the Supremes.

In contrast, Wells's post-Motown body of work featured only sporadic record releases over the next 20 years. None of her songs after "My Guy" approached the megasuccess of her Motown hits. After she left Hitsville, Mary Wells's career was widely regarded as washed up.

Dressed to the Motown standards of Maxine Powell, the head of the company's artist development program, Martha Reeves and the Vandellas pose for a publicity shot. Powell is credited with polishing the manners and dress of many of the young Motown stars like the Vandellas, whose first big hit was "(Love Is Like A) Heat Wave."

4

I Second That Emotion

ACCORDING TO GERALD Early, professor of African-American studies and author of *One Nation Under a Groove: Motown and American Culture*, Motown is probably the only major company in this country—and certainly the only major black-owned business—to ever establish itself as a true family for its employees. Motown is also the only independent record company to capitalize on a family-style image in order to achieve unprecedented commercial success.

"Our loyalty to one another and to our goals was so strong that the only reasonable description of that energy was something beyond business and beyond contracts—it was the sticking together that only happens in families," Berry explains in his foreword to *The Motown Album*, a coffee-table book rich with photos of 30 years in the life of the Motown family. "It doesn't matter what really accounted for our being perceived as a family, but I can tell you we all believed that we were. We certainly fought and loved like one. We would never have accomplished as much if that spirit had not existed."

This unique, communal spirit attracted some of the finest talent in Detroit to the busy Hitsville headquarters. In the 1960s Detroit was an absolute hotbed of musical talent, due in large part to the

Songwriters Brian and Eddie Holland teamed with Lamont Dozier to supply the musical genius for a seemingly unlimited number of hit singles. Holland-Dozier-Holland, or H-D-H, created top-of-the-chart songs for many Motown artists, including the Four Tops, Martha and the Vandellas, and the Supremes.

black community's strong emphasis on music education, both in the churches and in the schools. The Detroit public school system offered a well-regarded music program, and many of the kids who signed Berry's contracts had formed and rehearsed their bands while still in high school. The Miracles, the Temptations, and the Supremes were among them.

Berry took advantage of the musical genius that was blossoming all around him in Detroit by attending amateur performances at the local schools, including the one where he scooped up the Marvelettes. He would also spend late nights in the downtown clubs and theaters, continually on the lookout for talent. It was through his forays into the city's coolest jazz nightspots that Berry was able to build the backbone of Motown's music: the Funk Brothers backup band.

Bassist James Jamerson and drummer Benny "Papa Zita" Benjamin were both regular attractions at Detroit's hippest after-hours spots. Even later at night they would join keyboardist and bandleader Earl Van Dyke—and occasionally others, such as guitarist Robert White—in the close confines of the Hitsville studio. Although few fans outside Detroit knew all the players by name, this small group of jazz musicians became one of the most widely listened-to and danced-to bands in America. It was the Funk Brothers who played the music for Motown's many hits.

The in-house band did not typically tour with the Motown acts, instead remaining in Detroit at Berry's request. That way, the Funk Brothers were always on call for late-night Motown recording sessions. Berry paid his talented backup band handsomely for their loyalty, flexibility, and creativity. "In that time it was rare for a musician to own his own home, but I did," said Van Dyke. "Everybody there [at Hitsville] was buying Cadillacs. Everybody had some money. If you didn't come out of Motown with some money or some property, it wasn't Berry's fault."

Successful songwriters at Motown also did well for themselves. Brothers Brian and Eddie Holland first met Berry while still in their teens. Both eventually shelved their singing careers to focus on writing songs for Motown. Eddie teamed up with his younger brother when Brian's writing partner, Robert Bateman, left for New York, breaking up the Brianbert hit-making team. By early 1963 the Holland brothers had joined another young former singer named Lamont Dozier. Soon, Holland-Dozier-Holland, or H-D-H, began to demonstrate their gift for melody and their talent for creating storybook lyrics. Throughout the rest of the 1960s, H-D-H wrote an unprecedented number of hit singles, starting with "(Love Is Like A) Heat Wave" and "Quicksand" for Martha and the Vandellas; later, they crafted a string of million-dollar songs for both the Four Tops and the Supremes.

According to Dozier, the team often completed an amazing two or three songs in a single day, with Eddie writing the words, Brian creating the music, and Lamont contributing to both. "We would have parts of songs, like hooks [catchy, recurring vocal and instrumental lines] or maybe parts of a verse, so that by the end of the day we would have something accomplished," Lamont Dozier has explained. "I guess that was primarily the reason for the success we had in such a short time." In fact, H-D-H would prove to be one of the most prolific hit-producing teams in history.

Another reason for the three young songwriters' rapid and enormous success was the skill of the acts with whom they worked. The Four Tops, for example, probably the team's favorite Motown group, were seasoned performers with a history of successful nightclub appearances when they signed on at

Motown in 1963. Levi Stubbs, Abdul "Duke" Fakir, Lawrence Payton, and Obie Benson were from the same blue-collar Detroit neighborhood, a versatile, tight foursome who sang jazz on the local circuit before recording their first Motown music on Berry's Jazz Workshop label. Berry soon moved the Four Tops over to the Motown label, pairing them up with H-D-H to create such classic pop hits as "Baby I Need Your Loving," "I Can't Help Myself," and, later, "Standing in the Shadows of Love" and "Bernadette." Stubbs attributed the group's massive success to their gifted songwriting team: "Because of them, the Four Tops were the Four Tops. Without them, we couldn't get a hit."

Unlike most of the other popular acts at Motown, the Four Tops were not comfortable incorporating complicated dance steps into their stage act. Fakir defended their simple moves onstage by stating, "It came down to: What do you want me to do, sing or dance? We chose to concentrate on singing." But Berry enthusiastically encouraged Motown acts to use flashy stage moves, clever pantomime, and coordinated dance steps, eventually adding a choreography department to the artist development program at Motown. In 1965 dance instructor Cholly Atkins joined the staff.

As half of the legendary dance team Coles and Atkins, Cholly had traveled the world during the 1940s with fellow vaudeville tap dancer Charles "Honi" Coles before settling in New York and establishing himself as the choreographer for R&B groups appearing at the Apollo Theatre. In 1959 Cholly had worked with the Miracles on their dance steps after "Shop Around" became a hit. So, six years later, when Berry suggested that he join the Motown family, the dance instructor readily agreed. "The company was all black at that time and I very much wanted to see it grow," Cholly said later. "At that time we were very conscious of the

black movement and to be part of something destined to become a first and contribute to the future
of black artists was an opportunity."

After relocating to Detroit, Cholly introduced
his Hitsville students to a technique he called
"vocal choreography," which assisted the performers
with their breathing rhythms so that they could
step, strut, spin—and still have enough air to sing.
He also taught the Motown singers how to execute
the elaborate stage movements that eventually
became an integral component of black music performance: the swaying hands, the shimmies and
shakes, the synchronized dance steps, and the intri-
cate gestures to illustrate lyrics.

The Motown acts relied on Cholly for new

*Essential to every performance
was its stylized choreography
and flashy stage moves. Here
choreographer Cholly Atkins
leads the Four Tops in a
rehearsal of their stage routine;
he also helped mold the acts of
the Miracles and Temptations.*

choreography to match their newly released songs. "Semi-annually I had to revamp every act's show for when they went on the road," he recalls of his non-stop responsibilities at Motown. "Every time the company released a new single, that had to be integrated into the act. So whenever they were free I'd have them back in the studio working."

It was Cholly Atkins who helped mold Motown's most brilliant stage act, the Temptations. With the precision of a hip drill team, the tall, suave "Temptin' Tempts" would glide, dip, and slide across the stage, embellishing their catchy song lyrics with carefully orchestrated hand gestures and claps—all conducted in perfect unison. Impeccably dressed in colorful tuxes or sequined suits, the Temptations took the lessons they received at Motown's artist development program to heart, and it showed. But disruptive internal disagreements and serious personal problems would eventually diminish the worldwide success of this perfectly polished song-and-dance act.

Although the Temptations' lineup would shift and reshuffle itself regularly over the years, the group's five original members included Eddie Kendricks and Paul Williams from a trio called the Primes, plus high school chums Otis Williams, Melvin Franklin, and El Bryant of the Distants. The two R&B bands first met at a gig, where they admired each other's sophisticated harmonies and cool stage presence. When the five teenage singers teamed up, the new group named themselves the Elgins and auditioned at Hitsville for Berry, who immediately offered the young men a Motown contract.

After discovering that there was already another group at Motown called the Elgins, Otis Williams suggested a provocative substitute: "the Temptations." Once the handsome quintet realized, as Paul Williams put it, "We're selling sex," they began to capitalize on their undeniable charisma. "Those cats

Early members of the Temptations (front row: David Ruffin, who replaced original member El Bryant, Otis Williams; center: Eddie Kendricks; back row: Melvin Franklin, Paul Williams). It took a Motown contest, won by Smokey Robinson, to provide the group with its first hit single, "The Way You Do the Things You Do."

put on a show," recalls Dave Hamilton, the guitarist-vibist from Motown's travel band. "They worked. They worked hard. They sweated, you know, they'd be wringing out with sweat." They made all the right moves, using suggestive body language that made their female fans swoon. The Tempts were sizzling hot, especially after the dissatisfied and argumentative Bryant was replaced by Franklin's cousin, sexy solo artist David Ruffin. The lanky singer with the thick black eyeglasses had a rough, earthy-sounding voice and an astonishing amount of sex appeal onstage. With their dazzling stage presence and fancy footwork, the Temptations were a smash hit in concert. Yet the talented team failed to score even one hit single during their first three years in the Hitsville lineup.

From the time the group first auditioned at Hitsville in 1961, various Motown songwriters had tried unsuccessfully to create a hit song for the Tempts. Finally, in 1964, a company contest was held to entice the creative staff into producing that elusive top single. Berry penned a tune he thought might do the trick, but Smokey Robinson's "The Way You Do the Things You Do" won the Motown contest—and quickly shot up to the number 11 spot on the Top 40 hits chart. The song boosted the Temptations into the ranks of the Hitsville hit makers—where they belonged.

Over the next two years Smokey produced a number of classic hits for the slick singers, including "My Girl," the Temptations' first number one single, a million-seller and one of Robinson's sweetest ballads. But another ambitious young Motown songwriter named Norman Whitfield was angling for a chance to work with the Tempts; that chance materialized in 1966, when he came up with a winner. After the Tempts went to number 13 with "Ain't Too Proud to Beg," Whitfield emerged as one of Motown's most visionary songwriters.

Whitfield was an intense observer who had hung around Hitsville as a kid, virtually haunting the control room. Supporting himself by shooting a mean game of pool, the quietly persistent teen from Harlem slowly worked his way into a job in the quality control department, which "consisted of being totally honest about what [records] you were listening to," Whitfield told *Black Music* in 1976. He helped other Motown employees score the sample recordings, rating the records from one to ten and voting on which new songs deserved to be released. Whitfield was a quick study, and he believed that he would one day write great songs himself, surefire hits that would score well at the Friday-morning quality control meetings.

The songs Whitfield would produce for the Temptations—"Beauty Is Only Skin Deep," "(I Know) I'm Losing You," "You're My Everything," and "I Wish It Would Rain," among others—are sterling examples of the Motown Sound, the soulful pop music that Berry characterized in 1966 (in the liner notes for the Tempts' *Greatest Hits* album) as "the Sound of Young America." By this time much of Young America *had* embraced the Motown Sound—boys and girls, city kids and country kids, black kids and white kids. Only Motown could compete with the British Invasion and Beatlemania, or with America's own blond, beloved Beach Boys.

Between 1964 and 1967 Motown scored 14 number one pop singles and 46 more Top 15 pop singles—often beating out Beatles John, Paul, George, and Ringo for the top slot on the *Billboard* charts. As music critic Nelson George writes in *Where Did Our Love Go? The Rise and Fall of the Motown Sound*, "The Motown Sound was magical, it was fun, and it was lucrative. It was the sound of men who loved what they were doing, though to this day they still don't agree on just how it was done. All that is certain is that they made great music."

Between 1964 and 1967, Martha and the Vandellas topped the charts with "Dancing in the Street" and "Nowhere to Run." The Marvelettes scored a smash hit with "Don't Mess with Bill." Stevie Wonder, no longer "Little," made "Uptight (Everything's Alright)" into a classic. Marvin Gaye seduced audiences with "How Sweet It Is (To Be Loved by You)" and "Ain't That Peculiar." Saxophonist Autry DeWalt, of Junior Walker and the All Stars, who had joined Motown in 1964, climbed up the pop charts with such gritty, offbeat hits as "Shotgun" and "(I'm A) Road Runner." Jimmy Ruffin, older brother of the Temptations' lead

Berry Gordy in rehearsal with the Supremes (formerly known as the Primettes). Berry hoped to promote the young group as a crossover act—one that would appeal to older white audiences, as well as teenage America.

crooner, David, broke listeners' hearts with "What Becomes of the Brokenhearted." Even the relatively unknown Elgins had a hit with their classic "Heaven Must Have Sent You." At Motown in the mid-1960s, *everybody* was becoming a star.

In the meantime, Berry had begun a new campaign. He was determined to create and promote into superstardom the most famous crossover act in music history, a Motown act that would appeal to older white audiences as well as to teen America. He had selected for this honor a perky young girl group, the Primettes.

Years later Berry would admit that his choice of the Primettes stemmed from the fact that he had fallen in love with one of the young singers,

20-year-old Diane Ross. He eventually renamed her Diana (and her group the Supremes) in his obsessive crusade to make over the scrawny inner-city kid with the wispy voice and to transform her into America's most famous black songstress.

5

(Love Is Like A) Heat Wave

AT HITSVILLE THE employees' close working relationships—long days and late nights spent in intense intimacy—led to an ongoing soap opera of romances and marriages, breakups and divorces. Smokey Robinson married fellow Miracle Claudette Rogers in 1959; Marvin Gaye and Anna Gordy wed soon after them. Gwen Gordy married Motown's first production manager, former Moonglows crooner Harvey Fuqua. Loucye Gordy married Ron Wakefield, the saxophonist for Motown's touring band. One of the Marvelettes got married to one of the Miracles, another to a member of the Contours.

While still married to Ray, Berry fell for a beautiful but unstable teenager named Margaret Norton. Soon after separating from his wife, Berry fathered a child with Jeana Jackson, a friend from Connecticut, before Margaret Norton gave birth to their son, Kennedy, in the spring of 1964. By this time 34-year-old Berry had been divorced twice and was the father of six children—and he was wildly in love with Diana Ross.

"Women had been the inspiration of my life since childhood. They were what inspired me to do everything—create, make money, win," Berry says in *To Be Loved* of his Romeo reputation during the 1960s. "Now that I was winning, it was hard to turn

57

down the opportunities with women I seemed to have been working for all my life. I didn't."

When they first showed up at Hitsville in 1960, Diane Ross and the other Primettes—Florence Ballard, Barbara Martin, and Mary Wilson—were teenagers who lived in the Detroit projects. The Primettes sang gigs around town with the Primes, the quartet of male vocalists that included future Temptations Eddie Kendricks and Paul Williams. At their first audition for Motown, the Primettes were gently instructed by Berry to come back after they finished high school.

But "the girls," as Berry began to affectionately call them, were persistent. After a day of music classes, Diane would sew clothes and clean restaurant tables to earn money. Then she would rush over to Hitsville, where she and the other Primettes would hang out, volunteering to clap hands and sing backup for anyone who would let them. Other backup groups at Motown included the Andantes and three boys called the Love Tones. To create the driving backbeat that typified Motown songs, backup musicians would use wood blocks, two-by-fours, and, for "Dancing in the Street," tire chains!

Eventually, Berry gave in and signed the girls to a Motown contract. In their early days the newly named Supremes lacked finesse and the act floundered. When Barbara Martin left to have a baby, the loss only solidified the ambitious Diane's determination. "If the three of us can't make it, then we won't make it," she reportedly told Flo and Mary.

In late 1963 Berry assigned H-D-H to work with the girls. By July of 1964 "Where Did Our Love Go" had eased into the Top 40, sailing past the Beatles' "A Hard Day's Night" and the Beach Boys' "I Get Around" to reach the number one slot, where it remained for 13 weeks. H-D-H then produced for the Supremes four more consecutive number one hits: "Baby Love," "Come See About Me," "Stop! In the Name of Love," and "Back in My Arms Again." After a dip to number 11 with "Nothing but Heartaches," the Supremes were back on top of the pop charts again in 1965 with "I Hear a Symphony."

Over the next two years H-D-H would produce six more Top 10 hits for the Supremes, including the number one songs "You Can't Hurry Love," "You Keep Me Hangin' On," "Love Is Here and Now You're Gone," and "The Happening." Ranked as the third-hottest act of the '60s—trailing only the Beatles and Elvis Presley—the Supremes had become Motown's top priority. "Diane" became the more theatrical-sounding "Diana," and the three teens from the Detroit projects completed their caterpillar-to-butterfly transformation into the top female singing group in the United States.

While the trio worked on their style and stage presence with Maxine Powell and Motown's artist development program, Berry sent Diana off for extra tutoring at a predominantly white finishing school, the John Robert Powers School for Social Grace in downtown Detroit. The instructors at Powers taught the motivated but gawky young singer how to perform offstage, advising her to tone down her unladylike voice and makeup while playing up her natural beauty and charm.

As their catchy love songs became pop megahits, the Supremes were nurtured and encouraged, groomed and badgered into musical perfection— virtually sculpted into superstars. Although Diana received the bulk of the attention, she also bore the brunt of Berry's sharp critiques. But Berry gradually molded and scolded, pampered and pushed Diana Ross into embodying his ideal crossover pop-music icon; she responded by turning his vision into a history-making and extremely lucrative reality.

In order to win entrance into the "whites only" private clubs that dominated mainstream show business in the 1960s, Berry released a series of

Supremes albums that he hoped would expand their fan following. *The Supremes Sing Country, Western and Pop* and *Live at the Copa,* for example, were designed specifically to attract an adult audience to the trio's maturing talent and unusual versatility. But it was television that would launch the Supremes—and ultimately Motown—into the living rooms of white America.

Prior to the mid-1960s, pop musicians were not welcome guests on prime-time television. But by 1964 rock and roll and R&B dominated popular culture, making it impossible for TV executives to continue to ignore teen music. Dick Clark's afternoon show for teenagers, *American Bandstand*, was already hot; two other popular network dance programs, *Shindig* and *Hullabaloo*, soon followed. Yet, conservative TV executives would carefully screen artists before they appeared during prime time, restricting the acceptable performers to the biggest names and the most inoffensive acts—typically white singers who did not project overt sex appeal.

In December of 1964 the Supremes sang "Come See About Me" on *The Ed Sullivan Show*, television's most popular live entertainment program. Their TV debut wowed millions of Americans of all ages, colors, and income brackets.

Between 1965 and 1966 the Supremes sang on network TV 20 more times, making 6 widely-watched guest appearances on *The Ed Sullivan Show*. They became media darlings, not only gracing the covers of African-American publications like *Jet* and *Ebony*, but also appearing in the pages of *Look* and *Time* as well. Teens screamed, and the older folks tapped their feet. Even well-heeled music lovers who frequented the Copacabana and other exclusive nightclubs became big fans of the versatile pop singers, who made sure to incorporate American standards into their act: at Berry's insistence the Supremes sang jazz arrangements of Cole Porter songs

In 1965, Motown and its Tamla record label sponsored an international tour. Berry and three of his children accompanied the groups as the Motown Sound swept Germany, Holland, and France, as well as the United Kingdom.

and belted out Broadway melodies. Opening the door for other Motown acts, the Supremes appealed to virtually *everyone*, paving the way for future black crossover musicians and securing a place of respect for pop and soul music in American culture.

The international media fell in love with the young American trio, too, after British pop sensation Dusty Springfield hosted "The Sound of Motown," a London-based TV special featuring the Temptations, the Four Tops, Martha and the Vandellas, the Miracles, and the Supremes. Berry, his parents, and three of his children accompanied the acts on the set and for the remainder of their first international tour as the first transatlantic Motown

Revue spread the Motown Sound throughout Great Britain and on into Germany, Holland, and France. To everyone's surprise, Berry announced that after the tour he would remain in Paris for a few days of rest—with Diana.

When Berry and Diana returned to Detroit, their intense romantic involvement was no secret at Hitsville, where it served as added fuel for an already smoldering sense of employee dissatisfaction. The artists' incendiary list of complaints— about Berry's single-minded infatuation with Diana, among other things—had been ignored for too long. Now the in-house hostility was heating up to an unprecedented degree. In his autobiography Berry remembers that time as blissful: "When I look back on those years from 1965 to 1968 it seems we could do no wrong. The stream of hits was endless. The whole world was fast becoming aware of our overall success—our artists, our songs, our sound. I was being called the star maker, the magic man."

But behind his back at Motown, Berry was being called a lot of other, less complimentary names.

Raynoma Gordy Singleton, who had married a record producer in Washington, D.C., remembers noticing a change at Hitsville when she returned to Motown in 1967. "There was no longer a strong family atmosphere," she wrote in her autobiography. "The competition had turned into fighting, and the playful aggression was now actually overt hostility."

With the phenomenal rise of the Supremes and the huge success of so many other Motown acts, the company had outgrown its special family style of operation—and along with it, the Hitsville home base. By 1967 Berry had moved his offices into a downtown high-rise, an impersonal 10-story gray brick building. Hitsville continued to serve as a recording studio, and many of the artists still hung out there. But Berry was spending more time downtown with his savvy financial advisers, many of

whom were white. His blissful oblivious-
ness further increased his estrangement
from the Motown musicians and songwriters. Despite numerous warning signs
of an impending revolt, Motown's boss
continued to focus on Diana Ross—to the
exclusion of his other artists.

The Supremes were dealing with their
own set of divisive internal problems. In
the spring of 1967, when Berry made clear
his intention to make Diana a solo star,
the group's long-bubbling disharmony
began to boil over. Flo Ballard, who was
battling alcohol abuse and serious depres-
sion, was abruptly replaced by Cindy
Birdsong, a friend of Diana's. By the summer, club marquees announcing the
famous female trio publicized the biggest
change in the group: the girls were now
"Diana Ross and the Supremes."

By the time Martha and the Vandellas
racked up their sixth Top 10 hit with
"Jimmy Mack" in 1967, they felt that they
were being ignored at Motown—overshadowed by the unwavering spotlight
that was trained on Diana Ross. As their recording
sessions dwindled in number, Martha Reeves suffered a series of major depressions, and the group
eventually left Motown.

The Temptations, too, were wrestling with
internal strife, much of it stemming from David
Ruffin's mounting substance-abuse problems. After
he announced that he deserved top billing and
ordered the group to rename itself "David Ruffin
and the Temptations," Ruffin skipped one too many
gigs. In 1968 the Tempts voted Ruffin out, replacing
him with Dennis Edwards of the Contours. "To put
it bluntly," Otis Williams later said about the
group's popular but troubled former lead singer,

*Supremes (from left to right)
Mary Wilson, Diana Ross,
and Cindy Birdsong, perform
on the Ed Sullivan Show in
December 1967. In the spring
of that year Birdsong had
replaced Flo Ballard and by
summer the group's name had
changed as well—to "Diana
Ross and the Supremes."*

With Marvin Gaye, Tammi Terrell produced a string of hits in 1967 and 1968 such as "If I Could Build My Whole World Around You," "Ain't Nothing Like the Real Thing," and "You're All I Need to Get By." Terrell's death in 1970 from a brain tumor devastated her singing partner.

"success went to his head."

Smokey Robinson's wife, Claudette, had stopped touring with the Miracles at her doctor's suggestion in 1964. After suffering numerous miscarriages, Claudette decided to continue recording with the band but forgo the road trips. Despite long separations, made risky by Smokey's immense popularity with female fans, the marriage remained intact and the couple had two children, Berry and Tamla. By the late 1960s, however, Smokey wanted to quit the road, too. He was tired of the endless travel and the time spent away from his family. Nor could he overcome the increasing resentment he felt from the other members of his band, which Motown had renamed "Smokey Robinson and the Miracles."

One day Marvin Gaye expressed his seething dissatisfaction with the changes at Motown by instigating a brawl that culminated in a wild fistfight with Berry. In 1967 Marvin had teamed up with the petite, sexy Tammi Terrell for a series of smash-hit love duets, including "Ain't No Mountain High Enough," "Your Precious Love," and "If I Could Build My Whole World Around You." More hits followed in 1968 with "Ain't Nothing Like the Real Thing," and "You're All I Need to Get By." When his 22-year-old partner collapsed into his arms during a performance, Marvin was devastated. Although the two were not romantically involved (Marvin was still married to Anna Gordy, and Tammi was in love with David Ruffin), their friendship was deep and devoted. Diagnosed with a brain tumor, Tammi suffered until her death at age 24. Sensitive Marvin Gaye was never the same after she died.

Perhaps all the angry unrest at Hitsville during the late '60s was simply a reflection of the uneasiness that had seized the rest of the country. On July 23, 1967, a riot broke out in the ghettos of Detroit—just one of an estimated 164 riots that took place across the United States over the course of that long, hot summer. After a week of fires, looting, rock throwing, and machine-gun fire from the tanks and helicopters of the National Guard, 43 people lay dead in Detroit, 33 of them African Americans. It was the costliest race riot in history, the bloodiest in 50 years.

Miraculously, the Hitsville buildings were unscathed. But many of the surrounding homes and shops had been totally destroyed. Throughout the inner city entire blocks were gutted, everything burned to the ground. Tempers continued to flare after the riots were quelled, and the smell of smoke hung in the air of Detroit.

At Motown, Bobby Taylor of the Vancouvers brought his pet lion to work, and a black supremacist staff writer attacked a white executive with a machete. In the words of Raynoma Gordy Singleton, "Motown played the sounds of young America— pissed off. Bedlam."

6

What's Going On

A S THE TUMULTUOUS 1960s came to a close, the youth of America continued to rebel. Disgusted by what they called "the system," kids railed against the complacency of their parents with a government that waged senseless wars and allowed for inequality that separated men from women, rich from poor, blacks from whites. To illustrate their rejection of traditional American values, girls wore shockingly short miniskirts and let down their superlong, straight hair or let it grow into kinky Afros as big as the ones their black brothers wore. Young America turned up their stereos full blast, listening to music that expressed their disillusionment.

In 1968 and 1969 Motown spoke to the heart of young America. After his friend the Reverend Martin Luther King Jr. was assassinated, Berry released the album . . . *Free at Last*, a collection of inspirational speeches by the slain civil-rights leader. The Temptations grew Afros and sang "Cloud Nine," a hit single about the power of mind-altering drugs to dull the pain of living in the real world. (The song captured Motown its first Grammy Award in 1969.) Diana Ross and the Supremes tackled the issue of single motherhood with "Love Child" and "I'm Livin' in Shame."

Social unrest, demonstrations, protests, and riots divided the United States from the mid- to late 1960s. After wresting creative control of his music from Motown, Marvin Gaye responded to the chaos of the day, producing songs such as "Mercy Mercy Me (The Ecology)," "Inner City Blues (Make Me Wanna Holler)," and "What's Going On."

Smokey Robinson and the Miracles mourned the loss of America's most revered nonviolent leaders with "Abraham, Martin and John," a song composed in honor of Abraham Lincoln, Martin Luther King Jr., and John F. Kennedy—men shot down because of their efforts for racial equality.

Motown's artists and their songs continued to serve as a unifying force, giving voice to the social consciousness that characterized a new generation. In 1970 Edwin Starr, a relative newcomer to Motown, sang "War," an anti-Vietnam War diatribe with lyrics like, "War / What is it good for? / Absolutely nothin'!" The number one song became an anthem of the times. The Tempts hit the Top 10 with "Psychedelic Shack" and "Ball of Confusion (That's What the World Is Today)," songs that captured the chaotic feel of the era. Raw, edgy, electrifying music like the hits from Motown encouraged listeners to question the status quo and to work toward change.

Berry was determined to create a harmonious future—for himself and for his children, for Diana, and for Motown. Depressed by the despair and disrepair left in the ashes of the city he loved, Berry looked beyond Detroit. He wanted to move his business in order to extend Motown's unifying reach. Berry decided to expand his recording business into a multimedia production company, a venture that would be best accomplished in Hollywood.

Although Motown's move to Los Angeles did not become official until 1972, Berry began to make plans and connections. He wanted to work Motown songs into movies and Broadway productions, and into nationally televised specials. In 1968 Berry teamed up his two hottest acts when he paired Diana Ross and the Supremes with the Temptations to create the romantic Top 10 hit "I'm Gonna Make You Love Me." While the sensuous single was sweeping the United States, the two

Motown groups appeared together on the historic NBC special "TCB—Taking Care of Business: Diana Ross and the Supremes with the Temptations." Billed by one TV critic as "the first major black television special in history," the show captured a large audience. But Berry had even bigger plans for Motown.

When Berry first hired a 20-year-old booking agent from New York to be his creative assistant, he set her up in a Detroit office and paid her, but Motown's boss gave the brilliant young black woman absolutely nothing to do. Suzanne de Passe,

In 1968 the Temptations and Diana Ross and the Supremes performed on the Motown television special "TCB—Taking Care of Business." At the same time their joint single, "I'm Gonna Make You Love Me," reached the Top Ten hits list.

a college dropout from Harlem, rapidly took the initiative, becoming an indispensable adviser to Berry. Working long hours in the recording studio and going out on tour with the acts, the determined young dynamo continually updated Berry—who was spending more and more time in Los Angeles—on the latest developments in Detroit. Eventually, de Passe moved to Los Angeles to serve as the president of Motown Productions, Berry's TV and film entertainment division.

Meanwhile, Marvin Gaye was producing Motown's first great "concept" album (a series of songs linked by a central theme). His nine wrenching songs explored pressing social issues such as poverty, crime, and pollution, as well as the war in Vietnam. *What's Going On* would become the best-selling album in Motown history when it hit the airwaves in 1971. It was profound and prophetic—the masterpiece of Gaye's career. The jazz-influenced music and heartfelt lyrics reflected the *real* Marvin Gaye's soulful personality and world-weary soul.

Because *What's Going On* meant so much to Marvin, he fought hard for the album's release. Berry, who doubted that the sexy crooner could attract fans unless he sang romantic ballads, initially rejected the collection. But Marvin adamantly demanded that the work be released—or he would never again record for Motown. Berry's reluctant agreement paved the way for an unprecedented success—creative as well as financial—and inspired a push at Motown for top artists to take more control over their careers.

Stevie Wonder was one artist who paid close attention to the drama unfolding with Gaye. As soon as he turned 21, Stevie made his own musical statement: he produced his own album with help from his new wife, ex-Motown secretary Syreeta Wright. The couple then left Motown for New York, where Stevie further expressed his newfound creative freedom by experimenting with a relatively new instrument, the synthesizer.

The ethereal-sounding, often politically motivated songs he crafted for his first concept album, *Music of My Mind*, established Stevie Wonder as one of the most innovative artists of the 1970s. Fortunately for Motown, Stevie returned to his roots to cut the album. But he made sure that Motown paid up and provided him with a contract that guaranteed him total creative control—as well as more money than any Motown act had ever received.

Perhaps the artists would not have succeeded in changing the Motown system if Berry had spent more time at Hitsville. But the boss was distracted; he was building a new empire in California. Although the Motown family resented his absence, many artists also took advantage of it.

Motown Records had become a house divided: still pumping out the hits, but lacking in the unique intimacy and all-for-one unity that had helped make it the most successful black-owned business in America. Split in half, Motown kept its roots in Detroit while Berry was busy branching out into Hollywood.

In 1968 Berry purchased a sprawling, two-story Beverly Hills home that had belonged to comedian Tommy Smothers. Diana soon moved into a lovely mansion on the same star-studded, palm-lined street. Berry had already opened a California office that coordinated Hollywood-based Motown Productions, and Suzanne de Passe had introduced him to his next red-hot project: the Jackson 5.

Discovered by Bobby Taylor of the Vancouvers, the five young boys from Gary, Indiana, auditioned for Berry after Suzanne insisted, "You gotta hear these kids." Upon seeing a spirited performance by the ultratalented brothers, aged 9 to 17, Berry was immediately impressed with their discipline and professionalism. There was a quality about nine-year-old

Michael, Gordy would later explain, that grabbed his attention—"an unknown quality that I didn't completely understand but I knew was special. Somehow even at that first meeting he let me know of his hunger to learn, and how willing he was to work as hard as necessary to be great, to go to the top. He let me know he believed I was the person who could get him there."

In the spring of 1969 Berry moved the Jackson brothers to Los Angeles, where they rehearsed their act day and night. After getting kicked out of a series of rented apartments—where their late-night jams were not appreciated—the boys moved in with Berry. They also spent a lot of time at Diana's.

"In some ways, the three-ring circus that took over my home that summer in the Hollywood Hills reminded me of the old days at Hitsville," Berry recalled. "Music vibrating throughout the house, writing sessions on the floor of the living room, pep talks in the kitchen while eating, rehearsals through the midnight hours, impromptu baseball games at the nearby park, swimming, shooting pool, basketball. Camaraderie, creativity and, of course, competition." And there was romance, too: Berry's oldest daughter, 15-year-old Hazel Joy, fell in love with 17-year-old Jermaine Jackson. The two later married in a spectacular ceremony at the Beverly Hills Hotel.

The Jacksons became Suzanne de Passe's full-time assignment, and she rehearsed them daily, assisting in the choreography of their acrobatic stage moves. She even shopped for their cool-looking clothes. In 1971, after the Jackson 5 had won over the teenyboppers of America with a string of number one hits—"I Want You Back," "ABC," "The Love You Save," and "I'll Be There"—de Passe helped Berry orchestrate the boys' first television special. "Goin' Back to Indiana" proved to be Motown's greatest TV success to date, even more

popular than either "TCB" or its 1969 follow-up special, "GIT (Get It Together) on Broadway," which had again featured the Supremes and the Tempts. "Goin' Back to Indiana" was also more successful than "Diana!"—a musical spectacular aired earlier in 1971, in which Diana Ross had introduced the Jackson 5 to the American TV audience.

The boys from Indiana presented a dazzling, dynamic stage show that meshed perfectly with Berry's Hollywood dreams. The five Jacksons exuded wholesomeness and universal appeal. They represented an antidote to angry black militancy and a return to groovy but old-fashioned (and

The five Jackson brothers (front row: Marlon, Tito; back row: Jermaine, Michael, Jackie). The Jackson 5 signed with Motown in 1969 and soon became its most profitable act.

peaceful) fun. The Jackson 5 also signaled the end of the Motown record production line: the brothers were the last great act to emerge from Berry's hit factory. "I didn't realize that the launching of the Jackson 5 would mark the end of something major for me," Berry acknowledges in his autobiography. "They would be the last stars I would develop with the same intensity and emotional investment as I had with the earlier Motown artists. They would be the last big stars to come rolling off my assembly line."

While the Jackson 5 were making Top 100 history by becoming the first group whose first four singles hit number one, Diana Ross and the Supremes were ending their history-making run. After nearly a decade together the Supremes broke up, and Diana embarked on her solo career.

Jean Terrell replaced Diana after the group released its 12th—and last—number one song, "Someday We'll Be Together." The new Supremes immediately took off with two Top 10 hits, "Up the Ladder to the Roof" and "Stoned Love." Diana Ross, on the other hand, discovered that on her own she was an unknown entity.

Once Berry paired his superstar with the super-talented songwriting team of Nickolas Ashford and Valerie Simpson, however, the hits began flowing again. Ashford and Simpson had created virtually all the beautiful duets that climbed the charts for Marvin Gaye and Tammi Terrell. Using a similar fusion of gospel sound and poetic lyrics, the duo produced Diana's first five Top 40 hits as a solo act, starting with "Reach Out and Touch (Somebody's Hand)" in 1970.

After five years together Berry and Diana quietly ended their romance. In 1971 Diana surprised Berry and the rest of the world when she married Bob Silberstein, a handsome white public relations executive. But when Diana gave birth to a baby girl,

Diana Ross starred as the legendary jazz singer Billie Holiday in the 1972 Motown Productions film Lady Sings the Blues. *Ross had left the Supremes three years earlier in search of a solo career.*

Rhonda, less than nine months later, Berry sadly recognized the truth: the child was his. Diana did not tell her daughter until she neared her 13th birthday that "Uncle B. B." was actually her father.

In the meantime, Berry had formed a romantic partnership with Chris Clark, a tall, blond beauty with a soulful voice. Clark and Suzanne de Passe would go on to receive an Academy Award nomination for cowriting the screenplay for Motown's first movie, *Lady Sings the Blues* (1972), the story of legendary jazz singer Billie Holiday.

Motown had been established the same year that "Lady Day," as Billie Holiday was called, died.

Berry was an avid fan and had met the legendary African-American songstress at a Detroit nightclub just a year before her death. "The songs she sang all seemed to be about life—her life," Berry recalled. "I felt her pain was greater than any I had known. She was involved in a way of life I had not experienced and she told us about it."

Motown financed the multimillion-dollar movie, and Berry involved himself in every step of the film's creation, from early rehearsals to the double album soundtrack. Diana Ross starred in the film, playing Holiday as an abused teenager, a tough call girl, an up-and-coming jazz singer, and a heroin addict unable to pull herself out of a deadly whirlpool of personal pain. On the movie soundtrack Diana sang many of Holiday's signature songs, including "God Bless the Child" and "Good Morning Heartache." The soundtrack for *Lady Sings the Blues* went to number one on the pop charts before the movie was even released.

Ross was nominated for an Academy Award for Best Actress in early 1973; she won a Golden Globe Award for Most Promising Newcomer, along with much critical and popular acclaim. Although her other Motown films—the disappointing *Mahogany* in 1975 and *The Wiz,* which costarred Michael Jackson, in 1978—were box-office flops, Diana had become a major movie star. Berry was thrilled to have finally launched the ultimate black superstar, making good on one of his long-held dreams.

While Berry was engrossed in his Hollywood films, however, Motown's status as the leading African-American music label was rapidly falling to the huge corporate-controlled labels based in New York and Los Angeles. In 1973 Motown was cited by *Black Enterprise* magazine as the largest African American–owned company in America, grossing $40 million and employing 135 people. But by the mid '70s Motown was losing its stars as disgruntled songwriters and musicians left for other labels. *Lady Sings the Blues* marked the pinnacle of Motown's crossover success. The movie was also Berry's last major artistic triumph as his empire began to roll steadily downhill.

7

Money (That's What I Want)

A S THE "MAKE LOVE, not war" '60s evolved into the "make money" '70s and '80s, American businesses changed as well, setting the stage for an impersonal corporate culture that would come to dominate. Motown was not immune to nationwide shifts in social values and economic structure. The eventual demise of the Motown family would become a textbook example of the trend toward takeovers of the entertainment industry by conglomerates (large corporations formed when separate businesses consolidate).

When Gladys Knight and the Pips left Motown in 1973, they felt ignored and neglected by the very record company that had once reflected their own values. The Southern gospel-influenced group was indeed a family that stuck together: Gladys Knight and the Pips included Gladys and her brother Merald "Bubba" Knight, and their cousins Edward Patten and William Guest. The band, formed in 1952, had trained for years with Cholly Atkins to perfect its stage act before joining Motown in 1966. After hitting the top of the charts in 1967 with "I Heard It Through the Grapevine," the polished R&B act appeared in all the best clubs and theaters in the United States.

Despite Gladys Knight and the Pips' consistent

Berry Gordy related his story of Motown in the best-selling autobiography To Be Loved, *published in 1996. The book's title is the same as one of the five hits Berry composed for singer Jackie Wilson in the late 1950s.*

track record of hits—follow-up Top 10 singles included "Friendship Train," "If I Were Your Woman," and "Neither One of Us (Wants to Be the First to Say Goodbye)"— Gladys felt constantly overshadowed by Diana Ross. She was understandably pleased when her band decided to accept a lucrative offer from New York's Buddah Records.

Gladys Knight and the Pips were not the first to say good-bye to Motown; nor were they the last to leave. Martha Reeves and the Vandellas had parted ways with Motown a year earlier, eventually disbanding, as the Marvelettes had before them. The Four Tops were gone, too, recording for another label after their hit songwriting team, H-D-H, defected from Motown in 1968. "As Motown grew . . . they couldn't concentrate on everybody. They got *so* big. And so we just had to leave," explained the Tops' Lawrence Payton, voicing the sentiments of many of Motown's top artists.

By 1971 the Temptations had lost Eddie Kendricks, who quit the group to launch a brief solo career highlighted by two Top 10 hits ("Keep On Truckin'" and "Boogie Down"). Paul Williams, who was suffering from alcoholism and associated health problems, had reluctantly retired from the band. In 1973, following the massive success of their classic single "Papa Was a Rolling Stone," the Tempts learned that Paul Williams had shot himself. The original member of "the Temptin' Tempts" committed suicide only a few blocks from the old Hitsville studio. (Later, David Ruffin would die of a drug overdose, Kendricks of lung cancer, and Melvin Franklin of complications related to years of crippling arthritis masked by painkilling drugs. Of the original Temptations, only Otis Williams survives.)

After their hit songwriter Norman Whitfield was lured away by another record label, the Temptations' relationship with Motown deteriorated. Finally, in 1976 the disgruntled group left Detroit to sign with Atlantic Records. Unlike many other Motown artists, however, the Tempts would one day return to Motown and release another gold record: "Treat Her Like a Lady" was a Motown hit in 1984.

After 15 years with the Miracles, Smokey Robinson quit the group in 1972, pronouncing himself "burnt out." After reaching number one only once, with "Love Machine" in 1975, the Miracles disbanded in 1978. Smokey continued to write and record songs, moving to Los Angeles to assist Berry with the California branch of Motown. In 1979 Robinson scored big with his smooth single "Cruisin'." But by this time he was struggling with an all-too-common Hollywood pitfall: a debilitating cocaine addiction.

Although Smokey would bounce back, conquering his drug addiction to produce several more Top 10 songs during the 1980s, including the sensual "Being with You," Marvin Gaye was not so fortunate. After establishing himself in 1973 as the ultimate in sex appeal with his biggest-selling single, "Let's Get It On," Marvin's personal life fell apart. He grew paranoid from abusing drugs, Anna filed for divorce, and he had serious legal problems with the Internal Revenue Service, stemming from unpaid taxes. The troubled singer finally fled the country to live a reclusive life in Europe for a few years. After returning to the United States in 1982, Marvin Gaye released his last great hit, "Sexual Healing"—but not with Motown. His final Top 10 song appeared on the Columbia Records label. Two years later, in Los Angeles, Gaye's father shot and killed him during an argument. Berry Gordy and the rest of the world mourned the tragic loss of the soulful superstar.

Other early Motown stars who died tragically include the Supremes' Flo Ballard, who died an alcoholic and in poverty in 1976; Funk Brothers' James Jamerson and Benny Benjamin, both after decades of alcohol abuse; Paul Williams and David Ruffin of

A thrilled Marvin Gaye shows off one of two Grammy Awards won in 1982— for Best R&B Instrumental Performance and Best R&B Vocal Performance. Both honored his song "Sexual Healing" from the album Midnight Love, which was produced under the record label Columbia. Gaye had left Motown in 1981.

the Temptations; and Sandra Tilley of the Vandellas.

The Jackson 5 bid Motown good-bye to join CBS Records in 1975, after Michael's solo career took flight with five fast Top 40 hits. The Jacksons continued to appear on the Top 40 hits list while on CBS's Epic label, despite losing Jermaine (who remained at Motown with his wife, Hazel Joy Gordy) and Michael (who had signed as a solo artist with Epic). Over the next 10 years the youngest Jackson brother evolved into one of the most popular performers in the world, the kind of sensational African-American superstar Berry had envisioned when he first met nine-year-old Michael. According to Jackson, "Berry was my teacher and a great one. He told me exactly what he wanted and how he wanted me to help him get it."

After more than 20 years at Motown, Diana Ross signed with RCA in 1981. The year before, her last Top 10 solo hit at Motown was "It's My Turn." The pop tune was the title song for a movie of the same name, which starred Jill Clayburgh as a young woman trying to balance her career and romantic relationships.

Stevie Wonder remained at Motown, where he continued to create inventive music as well as the soulful romantic ballads Berry preferred, songs guaranteed to hit the Top 40. From the street-smart "Boogie On Reggae Woman" to 1981's "Happy Birthday"—which was adopted by the movement to make Martin Luther King Jr.'s birthday a national holiday—Wonder's consistently innovative sound represented the best of Motown. "There is nothing wrong with being part of an achievement of your culture," Stevie has said to explain his almost unwavering devotion to Motown through all of its changes.

Although most of the top acts from the early years at Hitsville had jumped ship, Motown sailed into the 1980s on a series of million-sellers, including back-to-back Top 40 hits by the Commodores. Discovered in the 1970s by Suzanne de Passe, who was a childhood friend of the group's manager, the Commodores buoyed the Motown roster during an era dominated by disco music. The group's wide range of sounds gave them mass appeal: they scored such diverse hits as the funky "Brick House" and the overtly sentimental "Three Times a Lady." Saxophonist Lionel Richie, who sang most of the leads, quit the Commodores in 1982 to become Motown's hottest solo artist of the decade.

Without Richie, the Commodores hit the Top 10

only once more, with "Nightshift" in 1985. Without the Commodores, Richie scored a dozen Top 10 hits over a span of five years. He struck gold for Motown with songs like "All Night Long (All Night)" in 1983 and "Say You, Say Me," the Oscar-winning love song from the 1985 film *White Nights*. Richie even made his own movie appearance in Motown's unpopular disco movie *Thank God, It's Friday* (1978).

In 1985 DeBarge, a young family group from Grand Rapids, Michigan, made its debut for Motown's film division. Led by 24-year-old El DeBarge, the group had its first Top 10 hit, "Rhythm of the Night," from the soundtrack for *The Last Dragon*, a martial arts film Berry produced that year. As a soloist, El DeBarge scored another Top 10 hit the following year on the soundtrack for *Short Circuit*, a popular kids' movie that was not a Motown production. But El DeBarge's celebrity was short-lived, and his songs faded from the airwaves.

One of Berry's own children also enjoyed a brief moment in the Motown spotlight. For several months in 1984, 19-year-old Kennedy Gordy's anthem to paranoia, "Somebody's Watching Me," was one of the top three songs in America. To keep the focus on his music instead of his parentage, Berry's son called himself Rockwell and occasionally broke into a British accent as he rapped the lyrics. Backup vocals were courtesy of childhood friend Michael Jackson.

During the 1970s and 1980s some of Motown's top hit makers were not African Americans. In the 1970s Motown's Rare Earth label recruited rock-and-roll bands, including the all-white rock sensation from Detroit called Rare Earth. But in the 1980s Teena Marie, a funk musician from Venice, California, claimed that her photograph did not appear on her Motown album because she was white.

Although actor Bruce Willis was also white, he was readily signed to Motown. Willis played a

raspy-voiced, street-smart private investigator on the popular television series *Moonlighting*. His bluesy Motown album *The Return of Bruno* sold a cool million copies. Willis's hit single from the album, a husky rendition of "Respect Yourself," was one of Motown's few Top 10 hits in 1987.

The Mary Jane Girls, Motown's interracial girl group, was produced by outrageous funk musician Rick James, who had scored his own Top 40 hit with "Super Freak." The "funk-and-roll" quartet hit the Top 10 in 1985 with "In My House."

Most of the Motown stars of the 1980s enjoyed only brief spins in the spotlight. In fact, in 1988 the only Motown record to make the Top 40 was the rerelease of a hit single from 1962. Featured in the hit movie *Dirty Dancing*, the Contours' "Do You

Motown artists Stevie Wonder and Lionel Richie joined with 46 rock and pop singers in January 1985 to raise funds for victims of famine in Africa. Helping to record the song "We Are the World" are USA for Africa members (clockwise left to right), Richie, Daryl Hall, Quincy Jones, Paul Simon, and Wonder.

Love Me" had originally been just one among hundreds of Motown's hot hits. Twenty-six years later, however, Berry was busy producing films instead of music. Preoccupied with his work in Hollywood, Berry was still very much aware of the accelerating decline of Motown's record division.

Although Motown remained at the top of *Black Enterprise* magazine's respected list of the top 100 black businesses in the United States and was still revered as the largest African-American company in history, Berry had developed serious financial problems by 1984. All of Motown's early TV specials had been well received, the company's investment in the hit Broadway musical *Pippin* had led to the release of a popular cast album, and the award-winning *Lady Sings the Blues* had marked Berry as a potential force in the film industry. But the five Motown movies that followed *Lady* had failed at the box office. And all of them had been immensely expensive. Without a strong roster of enduring Top 40 artists to balance out his Hollywood losses, Berry's empire was going down.

In 1983 Berry had sold Motown's distribution rights to MCA Records. His hand was forced by sweeping changes in the structure of corporate America. Conglomerate companies now made it almost impossible for independent labels like Motown to survive. Because the record giants—like CBS's Columbia and Epic; WEA's Warner Bros., Elektra, and Atlantic; PolyGram; RCA; MCA; and Capitol-EMI—had become so powerful, smaller music companies could no longer keep up. Berry could not compete with the big companies' multi-million-dollar artist promotions and massive record distribution networks. Motown was the last of the major independent labels, and it, too, was being eclipsed fast.

As head of Motown Productions, Suzanne de Passe created some superbly successful Motown-

themed TV specials, including the 1983 Emmy Award–winning spectacular "Motown 25: Yesterday, Today, Forever," in which Michael Jackson wowed viewers with his awesome moonwalk dance. "Motown 25" was the highest-rated musical special in the history of television, and de Passe followed it up in 1985 with another Emmy Award–winning special, "Motown Returns to the Apollo."

But Emmy Awards and ratings were not enough to save Motown, where the bottom line was still eroding as the company continued to lose millions of dollars. Berry was beginning to lose his motivation as well. "It was not only that we were losing money. I had lost interest," Berry admitted of his waning enthusiasm for the record industry tug-of-war that was destroying what was left of the independent

Television producer Suzanne de Passe (second from left) was honored at the Eighth Annual Black History Makers Awards Dinner in New York in 1994, along with (from left to right) publisher Edward Lewis, actress Ruby Dee, and poet laureate Maya Angelou. De Passe has high praise for Berry Gordy, who gave her the opportunity to reach the peak of her profession.

labels. "Selling wasn't just the right thing to do, it was the only thing to do," Berry had decided by 1988. The world had changed, and as Berry Gordy—by then the father of eight children and the grandfather of ten—later admitted, "I was just tired. I didn't want to do it anymore. It had long stopped being fun for me."

Although he had declined MCA Records' offer in December of 1986, Berry now accepted another, more generous deal. He turned over his rights to the Motown name, the Motown record catalog, and all the remaining Motown artists' recording contracts—in exchange for $61 million. Berry wisely retained all rights to his music publishing company, Jobete, thereby holding on to the publishing rights to virtually all the top Motown songs. He also kept his film and television company, which he renamed Gordy–de Passe Productions.

Only months before the sale was finalized, Berry was inducted into the Rock and Roll Hall of Fame along with the Supremes, followed by the Temptations and Stevie Wonder in 1989, and the Four Tops and H-D-H in 1990. (Smokey Robinson had been inducted in 1987. That same year Anna Gordy accepted the award for her late ex-husband when Marvin Gaye was honored posthumously.) The year after the sale Berry was honored by the Brotherhood Crusade with its prestigious Walter Bremond Pioneer of Black Achievement Award for "forever changing the record industry's attitude toward the value of Black music and entrepreneurial genius."

After a long relationship with a lovely blond named Nancy Leiviska, the mother of his eighth child, Stefan, Berry wed Grace Eaton, a young beauty of white and Asian ancestry with ankle-length ebony hair. At their Santa Barbara, California, wedding in 1990, guests included Diana Ross, Michael Jackson, Lionel Richie, and *Playboy* founder Hugh Hefner, Berry's former host for frequent evenings of serious backgammon games. Smokey Robinson and the Tempts' Melvin Franklin sang old Motown favorites for the large, star-studded gathering. The Gordys now live quietly in their Bel Air mansion, where Berry invests in racehorses and seems content to advise his large and ambitious family on a multitude of record and film production projects.

In 1997 Berry sold 50 percent of Jobete to EMI Music Publishing for $132 million, retaining his rights to the other half of the company's ongoing earnings. The most profitable arm of the Motown empire, Jobete continues to be a gold mine. Every time a song is played on the radio, on television, or in a movie, and every time it is performed, or "covered," by another artist, the music publisher earns royalties. Jobete published almost every Motown song until 1988. Not surprisingly, the publishing company's estimated value is more than $300 million.

PolyGram Records, which acquired Motown in 1993, has continued to market new records on Berry's old label. The current Motown roster still includes Stevie Wonder, the Temptations, and Diana Ross, but the label's biggest asset these days is the multiplatinum act Boyz II Men. PolyGram has yet to recoup its $300 million investment in the Motown name.

In his sale contract with MCA, Berry had stipulated that 20 percent of the ownership of Motown was to be earmarked for minorities to purchase, ensuring that Motown would live on—at least in part—as a black-owned label. As Berry's sister Esther told *Jet* magazine after the sale was made public in 1988, "I certainly understand the reaction of people who are very sad and say, 'Motown shouldn't be sold; it means so much to Black people.' But as you analyze the situation, you realize Berry Gordy has taken steps in the agreement to insure the Motown name will live on."

In 1998 actress Della Reese and business entrepreneur Berry Gordy Jr. were honored by the National Association of Black-owned Broadcasters. For his role in founding and running the Motown empire, which cultivated a music sound that crossed racial barriers, Gordy received a Lifetime Achievement Award.

A heartwarming collection of Motown memorabilia is housed in the original Hitsville studio on 2648 West Grand Boulevard in Detroit. Esther Gordy Edwards opened the original Motown Museum in 1980. Seven years later Hitsville was officially acknowledged with a state historical marker and renamed the Motown Historical Museum. When Esther renovated the museum in 1988, Michael Jackson donated $125,000 plus one of his infamous spangled gloves, which was lovingly tacked up on a Hitsville wall with a pushpin, in the old down-home Motown style.

When the immensely popular CBS television miniseries *Lonesome Dove* won Gordy–de Passe Productions seven Emmy Awards in 1989, Suzanne de Passe reached the top of Hollywood's predominantly white male hierarchy. At the time she was the only black woman to head a major Hollywood production company. Praising her former boss, de Passe told a journalist at *Harper's Bazaar* in 1985, "Men own the ballpark, men own the team, and we get to play. Never, not even when the going was rough, did Berry make me sit on the bench because I was a woman." She later told *Time* magazine, "I was planted in a garden that allowed me to grow."

Suzanne de Passe went on to plant her own garden when she formed the de Passe Entertainment Company. *The Temptations*, her 1998 NBC miniseries about the rise, fall, and resurrection of the talented and troubled Motown supergroup, has been one of her most successful projects. Another de Passe miniseries aired on ABC that same year: an intimate four-hour documentary, *Motown 40: The Music Is Forever* tells the compelling story of the rise and fall of the Motown family empire.

An American institution, the Motown Sound lives on, deeply rooted in the heartbeat of popular music. The realization of one man's dream, Motown will always remain a testament to the ability of African-American artists to change the course of history and popular culture.

Surrounded by Motown legends (from left to right) Stevie Wonder, Otis Williams of the Temptations, Smokey Robinson, and Diana Ross, Berry Gordy accepts a star on the Hollywood Walk of Fame from Mayor Johnny Grant, on October 24, 1996.

1929   Berry Gordy Jr. born in Detroit, Michigan, on November 28

1953   Opens the 3D Record Mart; marries Thelma Coleman

1955   The 3D Record Mart folds; Berry works on the assembly line at Ford's Lincoln-Mercury plant

1957   Quits Ford and cowrites first hit song, "Reet Petite"; meets Smokey Robinson

1959   Berry and Thelma divorce; he forms Jobete Music Publishing; moves into Hitsville U.S.A.; creates Tamla and Motown record labels

1960   Berry marries Raynoma "Ray" Liles; Motown scores first Top 10 hit, "Shop Around"

1961   Motown's first successful girl group, the Marvelettes, records the label's first number one song, "Please Mr. Postman"; Diane Ross and the Primettes sign up at Motown and become the Supremes

1962   Mary Wells becomes Motown's first solo superstar with three Top 10 hits; Motortown Revue is launched; Berry and Ray divorce

1963   Marvin Gaye and Little Stevie Wonder score their first Top 10 hits; Martha and the Vandellas hit Top 10 with "(Love Is Like A) Heat Wave"; Berry records first album of speeches by the Reverend Martin Luther King Jr.

1964   The Motown Sound challenges the British Invasion with Top 40 hits by the Supremes, the Temptations, and the Four Tops; the Supremes appear on *The Ed Sullivan Show*; Mary Wells leaves Motown

1965   Cholly Atkins joins Maxine Powell in Motown's Artist Development Department; Motown Revue tours Europe

1967   Marvin Gaye and Tammi Terrell team up; the Supremes become "Diana Ross and the Supremes"; Berry opens another office in downtown Detroit; riots devastate inner city of Detroit

1968   Suzanne de Passe joins Motown; TV special "TCB" airs nationally; the Jackson 5 audition at Motown

CHRONOLOGY

1969   Motown's "GIT (Get It Together) on Broadway" airs on TV; the Temptations' "Cloud Nine" wins Motown's first Grammy Award; Diana Ross leaves the Supremes; the Jackson 5 sing their first Top 40 hit

1970   Tammi Terrell dies

1971   "Goin' Back to Indiana" airs on network TV; Marvin Gaye's *What's Going On* becomes Motown's best-selling album; Stevie Wonder signs new Motown contract

1972   Motown moves to Los Angeles; *Lady Sings the Blues* wins acclaim for Diana Ross and Motown Productions

1973   Motown cited in *Black Enterprise* as biggest black-owned business in United States; Gladys Knight and the Pips leave Motown; Paul Williams of the Temptations commits suicide

1975   Diana Ross stars in Motown's *Mahogany*; the Jackson 5 leave Motown

1976   The Temptations leave Motown

1978   Motown Productions releases *Almost Summer*; *Thank God, It's Friday*; and *The Wiz*

1979   Smokey Robinson has first solo hit with "Cruisin'"

1980   Esther Gordy Edwards opens Motown Museum at old Hitsville U.S.A. studio

1981   Suzanne de Passe becomes president of Motown Productions; Diana Ross leaves Motown for RCA

1982   Lionel Richie begins string of Top 10 hits for Motown

1983   NBC airs "Motown 25: Yesterday, Today, Forever"; Berry signs over distribution rights to MCA Records

1984   Marvin Gaye is shot and killed by his father

1985   Motown releases *The Last Dragon*; airs TV special "Motown Returns to the Apollo" and two Motown-based TV series

1988   Berry is inducted into Rock and Roll Hall of Fame; the Contours' rerelease of "Do You Love Me" is Top 40 hit again after 26 years; Berry sells Motown to MCA Records

1989   Berry receives Brotherhood Crusade's Walter Bremond Pioneer of Black Achievement Award; CBS airs Gordy and de Passe's *Lonesome Dove* miniseries

1990   Berry Gordy marries Grace Eaton

1991   Boyz II Men cut Motown label hit "Motownphilly"

1993   PolyGram buys Motown

1997   Berry sells 50 percent of Jobete to EMI

1998   De Passe Entertainment releases *The Temptations*; ABC airs *Motown 40: The Music Is Forever*

SELECTED DISCOGRAPHY

The following listing includes (in order of their release) some of the many top-selling records (mostly hit singles) produced by Berry Gordy's Motown Records.

YEAR	SONG	PERFORMER(S)
1960	"Shop Around"	The Miracles
1961	"Please Mr. Postman"	The Marvelettes
1962	"Do You Love Me"	The Contours
	"Twistin' Postman"	The Marvelettes
	"The One Who Really Loves You"	Mary Wells
	"You Beat Me to the Punch"	Mary Wells
	"Two Lovers"	Mary Wells
	"Playboy"	The Marvelettes
	"Beechwood 4-5789"	The Marvelettes
1963	"Hitch Hike"	Marvin Gaye
	"You've Really Got a Hold on Me"	The Miracles
	"(Love Is Like A) Heat Wave"	Martha and the Vandellas
	"Pride and Joy"	Marvin Gaye
	"Fingertips (Part 2)"	Little Stevie Wonder
	"Quicksand"	Martha and the Vandellas
	"Can I Get a Witness"	Marvin Gaye
	The Great March to Freedom (album)	Rev. Martin Luther King Jr. (speeches)
1964	"My Guy"	Mary Wells
	"Dancing in the Street"	Martha and the Vandellas
	"The Way You Do the Things You Do"	The Temptations
	"Baby I Need Your Loving"	The Four Tops
	"Where Did Our Love Go"	The Supremes
	"Baby Love"	The Supremes
	"Come See About Me"	The Supremes
	"How Sweet It Is (To Be Loved by You)"	Marvin Gaye

YEAR	SONG	PERFORMER(S)
1965	"Nowhere to Run"	Martha and the Vandellas
	"My Girl"	The Temptations
	"Stop! In the Name of Love"	The Supremes
	"Back in My Arms Again"	The Supremes
	"I Can't Help Myself"	The Four Tops
	"Nothing but Heartaches"	The Supremes
	"I Hear a Symphony"	The Supremes
	"Shotgun"	Junior Walker and the All Stars
	"The Tracks of My Tears"	The Miracles
	"It's the Same Old Song"	The Four Tops
	"Ain't That Peculiar"	Marvin Gaye
1966	"Don't Mess with Bill"	The Marvelettes
	"My World Is Empty Without You"	The Supremes
	"Uptight (Everything's Alright)"	Stevie Wonder
	"Love Is Like an Itching in My Heart"	The Supremes
	"You Can't Hurry Love"	The Supremes
	"Reach Out I'll Be There"	The Four Tops
	"Ain't Too Proud to Beg"	The Temptations
	"I'm Ready for Love"	Martha and the Vandellas
	"You Keep Me Hangin' On"	The Supremes
	"Beauty Is Only Skin Deep"	The Temptations
	"(I Know) I'm Losing You"	The Temptations
	"What Becomes of the Brokenhearted"	Jimmy Ruffin
	"(I'm A) Road Runner"	Junior Walker and the All Stars
	"Standing in the Shadows of Love"	The Four Tops
	"Heaven Must Have Sent You"	The Elgins
1967	"Ain't No Mountain High Enough"	Marvin Gaye and Tammi Terrell
	"I Was Made to Love Her"	Stevie Wonder
	"Love Is Here and Now You're Gone"	The Supremes

SELECTED DISCOGRAPHY

YEAR	SONG	PERFORMER(S)
1967	"I Second That Emotion"	Smokey Robinson and the Miracles
	"Jimmy Mack"	Martha and the Vandellas
	"Your Precious Love"	Marvin Gaye and Tammi Terrell
	"If I Could Build My Whole World Around You"	Marvin Gaye and Tammi Terrell
	"All I Need"	The Temptations
	"You're My Everything"	The Temptations
	"Bernadette"	The Four Tops
	"The Happening"	The Supremes
	"Reflections"	Diana Ross and the Supremes
	"I Heard It Through the Grapevine"	Gladys Knight and the Pips
1968	"I Wish It Would Rain"	The Temptations
	"Ain't Nothing Like the Real Thing"	Marvin Gaye and Tammi Terrell
	"For Once in My Life"	Stevie Wonder
	. . . Free At Last (album)	Rev. Martin Luther King Jr. (speeches)
	"You're All I Need to Get By"	Marvin Gaye and Tammi Terrell
	"Cloud Nine"	The Temptations
	"Love Child"	Diana Ross and the Supremes
	"I'm Gonna Make You Love Me"	Diana Ross and the Supremes and the Temptations
1969	"I'm Livin' in Shame"	Diana Ross and the Supremes
	"My Cherie Amour"	Stevie Wonder
	"Abraham, Martin and John"	Smokey Robinson and the Miracles
	"Friendship Train"	Gladys Knight and the Pips
	"I Can't Get Next to You"	The Temptations
	"Someday We'll Be Together"	Diana Ross and the Supremes
	"I Want You Back"	The Jackson 5
1970	"ABC"	The Jackson 5

YEAR	SONG	PERFORMER(S)
1970	"Psychedelic Shack"	The Temptations
	"The Love You Save"	The Jackson 5
	"I'll Be There"	The Jackson 5
	"War"	Edwin Starr
	"Up the Ladder to the Roof"	The Supremes (without Diana Ross)
	"The Tears of a Clown"	Smokey Robinson and the Miracles
	"Ball of Confusion (That's What the World Is Today)"	The Temptations
	"Signed, Sealed, Delivered, I'm Yours"	Stevie Wonder
	"It's a Shame"	The Spinners
	"Get Ready"	Rare Earth
	"If I Were Your Woman"	Gladys Knight and the Pips
	"Reach Out and Touch (Somebody's Hand)"	Diana Ross
	"Stoned Love"	The Supremes
1971	"Stop the War Now"	Edwin Starr
	"Just My Imagination (Running Away with Me)"	The Temptations
	"What's Going On"	Marvin Gaye
	"Superstar (Remember How You Got Where You Are)"	The Temptations
	"Never Can Say Goodbye"	The Jackson 5
	"Got to Be There"	Michael Jackson
1972	"Rockin' Robin"	Michael Jackson
	"Ben"	Michael Jackson
	"Superstition"	Stevie Wonder
	"Papa Was a Rolling Stone"	The Temptations
1973	"Let's Get It On"	Marvin Gaye
	"You Are the Sunshine of My Life"	Stevie Wonder

SELECTED DISCOGRAPHY

YEAR	SONG	PERFORMER(S)
1973	"Neither One of Us (Wants to Be the First to Say Goodbye)"	Gladys Knight and the Pips
	"Keep On Truckin' (Part I)"	Eddie Kendricks
	"Living for the City"	Stevie Wonder
1974	"Boogie Down"	Eddie Kendricks
	"Don't You Worry 'Bout a Thing"	Stevie Wonder
	"Boogie On Reggae Woman"	Stevie Wonder
	"Machine Gun"	The Commodores
1975	"Love Machine (Part I)"	The Miracles (without Smokey Robinson)
	"Theme from Mahogany (Do You Know Where You're Going To)"	Diana Ross
1976	"Sweet Love"	The Commodores
	"Just to Be Close to You"	The Commodores
	"I Wish"	Stevie Wonder
	"Love Hangover"	Diana Ross
1977	"Sir Duke"	Stevie Wonder
	"Easy"	The Commodores
	"Brick House"	The Commodores
1978	"Three Times a Lady"	The Commodores
1979	"Sail On"	The Commodores
	"Still"	The Commodores
	"Cruisin'"	Smokey Robinson
1980	"Upside Down"	Diana Ross
	"I'm Coming Out"	Diana Ross
	"Master Blaster (Jammin')"	Stevie Wonder
	"It's My Turn"	Diana Ross
1981	"I Need Your Lovin'"	Teena Marie
	"Being with You"	Smokey Robinson

YEAR	SONG	PERFORMER(S)
1981	"Happy Birthday"	Stevie Wonder
	"Super Freak"	Rick James
	"Lady (You Bring Me Up)"	The Commodores
1982	"That Girl"	Stevie Wonder
	"Truly"	Lionel Richie
1983	"You Are"	Lionel Richie
	"My Love"	Lionel Richie
	"All Night Long (All Night)"	Lionel Richie
	"Running with the Night"	Lionel Richie
1984	"Hello"	Lionel Richie
	"Stuck on You"	Lionel Richie
	"Penny Lover"	Lionel Richie
	"I Just Called to Say I Love You"	Stevie Wonder
	"Treat Her Like a Lady"	The Temptations
1985	"Nightshift"	The Commodores (without Lionel Richie)
	"In My House"	Mary Jane Girls
	"Part-Time Lover"	Stevie Wonder
	"Say You, Say Me"	Lionel Richie
	"Rhythm of the Night"	DeBarge
1986	"Dancing on the Ceiling"	Lionel Richie
	"Who's Johnny"	El DeBarge
	"Love Will Conquer All"	Lionel Richie
1987	"Ballerina Girl"	Lionel Richie
	"Respect Yourself"	Bruce Willis
	"Just to See Her"	Smokey Robinson
	"One Heartbeat"	Smokey Robinson
	"Se La"	Lionel Richie
1988	"Do You Love Me" (rerelease)	The Contours

SELECTED DISCOGRAPHY

THE GRAMMY HALL OF FAME

The Recording Academy, established in 1957, annually presents its most prestigious award, the Grammy Award, to recognize notable achievement in the recording industry. In 1973, the organization's National Trustees decided to honor recordings "of lasting, qualitative, or historical significance . . . released more than 25 years ago" by placing them within a Grammy Hall of Fame. Several rhythm and blues (R&B) and pop recordings made under the Motown and Tamla record labels received this recognition in the late 1990s:

SINGLES

"Ain't No Mountain High Enough"
Marvin Gaye and Tammi Terrell
(Tamla, 1967) R&B

"I Heard It Through the Grapevine"
Marvin Gaye (Tamla, 1968) R&B

"I Want You Back"
Jackson 5 (Motown, 1969) Pop

"My Guy"
Mary Wells (Motown, 1964) R&B

"Reach Out I'll Be There"
Four Tops (Motown, 1966) R&B

"Superstition"
Stevie Wonder (Tamla, 1972) R&B

"Where Did Our Love Go?"
The Supremes (Motown, 1964) Pop

"You Keep Me Hangin' On"
The Supremes (Motown, 1966) Pop

"You've Really Got a Hold on Me"
The Miracles (Tamla, 1963) R&B

ALBUMS

Innervisions
Stevie Wonder (Tamla, 1973) R&B

Talking Book
Stevie Wonder (Tamla, 1972) R&B

What's Going On
Marvin Gaye (Tamla, 1971) R&B

Source: The Recording Academy: The Grammy Hall of Fame
http://www.grammy.com/awards/hall.html

The following television programs and motion pictures were produced by Berry Gordy's Motown Productions.

TELEVISION

1968   "TCB—Taking Care of Business: Diana Ross and the Supremes with the Temptations" (special)

1969   "GIT (Get It Together) on Broadway" (special, starring Diana Ross and the Supremes and the Temptations)

1971   "Diana!" (special, starring Diana Ross and introducing the Jackson 5)

1971   "Goin' Back to Indiana" (special, starring the Jackson 5)

1977   *Scott Joplin* (movie)

1983   "Motown 25: Yesterday, Today, Forever" (special)

1985   "Motown Returns to the Apollo" (special)

1985   *The Motown Revue* (series, hosted by Smokey Robinson)

1985   *Motown on Showtime* (series)

1989   *Lonesome Dove* (miniseries)

MAJOR MOTION PICTURES

1972   *Lady Sings the Blues*

1975   *Mahogany*

1976   *The Bingo Long Traveling All-Stars and Motor Kings*

1978   *Almost Summer*

1978   *Thank God, It's Friday*

1978   *The Wiz*

1985   *The Last Dragon*

BIBLIOGRAPHY

Beller, Miles. "Making Motown's Movies." *Harper's Bazaar*, September 1985.

Bianco, David. *Heat Wave: The Motown Fact Book*. Ann Arbor, Mich.: Pierian Press, 1989.

"Brotherhood Crusade Salutes Motown's Berry Gordy." *Jet*, 30 January 1989.

Castro, Janice. "Hitsville Goes Hollywood." *Time*, 30 January 1989.

Cox, Ted. *The Temptations*. Philadelphia: Chelsea House Publishers, 1997.

De Curtis, Anthony, and James Henke, eds. *The Rolling Stone Illustrated History of Rock and Roll*. New York: Random House, 1992.

Early, Gerald. *One Nation Under a Groove: Motown and American Culture*. Hopewell, N.J.: Ecco Press, 1995.

Fong-Torres, Ben. *The Motown Album*. New York: St. Martin's Press, 1990.

George, Nelson. *Where Did Our Love Go? The Rise and Fall of the Motown Sound*. New York: St. Martin's Press, 1985.

Gordy, Berry. *To Be Loved: The Music, the Magic, the Memories of Motown*. New York: Warner Books, 1994.

Marsh, Dave, ed. *Women of Motown: An Oral History*. New York: Avon, 1998.

"MCA/Boston Ventures Buy Motown for $61 Million." *Jet*, 18 July 1988.

Morse, David. *Motown*. New York: Collier Books, 1971.

Pareles, Jon, and Patricia Romanowski, eds. *The Rolling Stone Encyclopedia of Rock and Roll*. New York: Rolling Stone Press/Summit Books, 1983.

Powell, Maxine, and Julie Greenwalt. "Rock 'n' Role Model." *People Weekly*, 13 October 1986.

Ritz, David. "Soul Serenade." *TV Guide*, 14 February 1998.

Singleton, Raynoma Gordy. *Berry, Me, and Motown: The Untold Story*. Chicago: Contemporary Books, 1990.

Whitburn, Joel. *The Billboard Book of Top 40 Hits*, 6th edition. New York: Billboard Books, 1996.

BOOKS

Bianco, David. *Heat Wave: The Motown Fact Book*. Ann Arbor, Mich.: Pierian-Press, 1989.

Cox, Ted. *The Temptations*. Philadelphia: Chelsea House Publishers, 1997.

De Curtis, Anthony, and James Henke, eds. *The Rolling Stone Illustrated History of Rock and Roll*. New York: Random House, 1992.

Fong-Torres, Ben. *The Motown Album*. New York: St. Martin's Press, 1990.

Gordy, Berry. *To Be Loved: The Music, the Magic, the Memories of Motown*. New York: Warner Books, 1994.

Hardy, James Earl. *Boyz II Men*. Philadelphia: Chelsea House Publishers, 1999.

Horwich, Richard, ed. *Michael Jackson*. New York: Gallery Books, 1984.

Marsh, Dave, ed. *Women of Motown: An Oral History*. New York: Avon, 1998.

Mussari, Mark. *Suzanne de Passe: Motown's Boss Lady*. Ada, Okla.: Garrett Educational Corporation, 1992.

Ritz, David. *Divided Soul: The Life of Marvin Gaye*. New York: McGraw-Hill, 1991.

Taraborrelli, J. Randy. *Call Her Miss Ross*. Secaucus, N.J.: Carol Publishing Group, 1989.

Whitburn, Joel. *The Billboard Book of Top 40 Hits*, 6th edition. New York: Billboard Books, 1996.

FURTHER READING

WEBSITES

The Motown Historical Museum
http://recordingeq.com/motown.htm

Motown at 40 Presented by the Detroit Free Press
http://www.motownat40.com

The Motown Record Company
http://www.motown.com

The Motown Webring
http://welcome.to/the-motown-webring

Rock and Roll Hall of Fame and Museum
http://www.rockhall.com/

INDEX

PICTURE CREDITS

VIRGINIA ARONSON is the author of more than 24 books, many of them for young people. She has written several books for Chelsea House, including the GALAXY OF SUPERSTARS biography *Venus Williams*. She lives with her husband and their young son in South Florida, where they like to blast old Motown records on the stereo.